ENABLE

QUEEN OF THE TURF

ENABLE

QUEEN OF THE TURF

EDITED BY ANDREW PENNINGTON

RACING POST
— LEGENDS —

First published by Pitch Publishing on behalf of Racing Post, 2021

Pitch Publishing
A2 Yeoman Gate
Yeoman Way
Worthing
Sussex
BN13 3QZ
www.pitchpublishing.co.uk

info@pitchpublishing.co.uk

www.racingpost.com/shop

A CIP catalogue record is available for this book from the British Library.

ISBN 9781785318375

Typesetting by John Schwartz
Printed and bound in Slovenia by DZS Grafik, Ljubljana

Photographic acknowledgements
All the photos are copyright Racing Post except the following:
Getty Images pages 2, 10-11, 16, 52, 55, 58-59, 79, 81, 83, 104, 114, 161
Grossick Racing page 12

Frontispiece: Frankie Dettori gives Enable an affectionate pat after their Yorkshire Oaks victory in August 2019

CONTENTS

FOREWORD

by Brough Scott

THEY TOOK us on a journey never matched before. No horse and rider have ever blazed an international trail to equal that by Enable and Frankie Dettori. From Epsom to Ascot to Ireland to America and so gloriously but also painfully to Paris, their 11 Group 1s are seared in the memory. This book is to try and capture some of the sunshine that they spread.

Mind you, it was biblical thunder and lightning through which her brilliance first shone. I remember standing on the ITV rostrum as we digested what she had done to her Oaks rivals at Epsom and saying 'that was the race of the season'. Ah, but there were so many more to come.

The dominance of that first season, ending with that power-packed victory in the Chantilly Arc. The injury scare of the second, the reaching-for-the-line Arc at Longchamp followed by the Breeders' Cup triumph in Kentucky. The Eclipse success to start the third followed by that greatest of Ascot duels in the King George and, just when a third Arc seemed in her grasp, the avenging angel that was Waldgeist nailing her at the death.

So we were rewarded with that fourth season and by now It was not just Frankie and Enable, John Gosden, Khalid Abdullah and Teddy Grimthorpe. It was all the backroom team. Imran Shahwani and Tony Proctor at her head for the races, Helen who was in charge of her barn, assistant trainer Barry O'Dowd for whom this was the best of all the horses he had handled at Clarehaven.

We came to share their delight and, of course, to share in the heartbreak of those two gallant losing days at Longchamp. A third

Opposite page: John Gosden saddles Enable before her second success in the Yorkshire Oaks in August 2019

Enable works on the Limekilns gallop in Newmarket six days before the Prix de l'Arc de Triomphe in September 2019

Arc would have been nothing less than the supreme moment in racing history. Victory would put her and Frankie out into the stratosphere and would leave something unique in the memory of the millions yearning for this ultimate of coronations. Oh how she tried on that rain-soaked Parisian turf. But it was not to be.

In some ways that makes her story even better. Enable was not a machine, she was equine flesh and blood that for four seasons had put her mind and body on the line to give us inspiration. She was the fourth generation and finest product of the thoroughbred families so scrupulously studied by Khalid Abdullah and reared with such care by the Juddmonte team in Ireland and in her and Frankel's birthplace at Banstead Manor. How sweet a coincidence that it should have also been the happiest of childhood homes to Winston Churchill.

Training the racehorse is about empathy, efficient structures and, most of all, about judgement calls. Enable's success was the ultimate proof of John Gosden's absolute mastery of that profession just as her transatlantic, four-country, 11 Group 1-race victories made Frankie Dettori feel more for her than any other horse in his unparalleled 33-season career.

The Racing Post has followed Enable and the team around her every step of the way. These pages are no more and no less than a scrapbook, an at-the-time witness to the growing realisation that among us was one of the greatest animals to ever tread the turf, that 300 years of selective breeding and several much more recent lifetimes of effort had not been in vain.

Read on and enjoy. This is the story of how Enable became, and will always remain, a horse for the ages.

BROUGH SCOTT
October 2020

ONE

EARLY DAYS

Previous spread: Frankie Dettori enjoys his first victory on Enable in the Cheshire Oaks at Chester in May 2017

ENABLE WAS A blueblood of the highest order hailing as she did from a Juddmonte family stretching back nearly 40 years and, like her illustrious predecessor Frankel, was broken in at Khalid Abdullah's Ferrans Stud in County Meath.

That process went smoothly and she was among the first batch of Juddmonte's 2014 homebred crop to be sent into training. In February 2016 she joined John Gosden at his Clarehaven Stables in Newmarket.

Gosden was happy to take his time with Enable during the course of 2016 as she settled into her new surroundings and he was finally ready to introduce the daughter of Nathaniel at the end of November on the all-weather at Newcastle. She impressed seasoned racewatchers with her winning performance at Gosforth Park when beating eight rivals by upwards of three and three-quarter lengths.

Jockey Robert Havlin was also taken with her victory, saying: 'Enable is a nice filly. She did that well, though I don't think there was much strength to the race, but she could do no more than win. I expect she will be put away until next season when she will probably start off over a mile and a quarter.'

Enable makes an impressive winning debut under Robert Havlin on Newcastle's all-weather track in November 2016

RACING POST ANALYSIS – **ASHLEY RUMNEY**

Enable, a half-sister to a Group-placed filly and a three-time all-weather winner, knew her job on this debut and settled the issue pretty quickly before drawing away to score comfortably. She looks capable of going on to better things.

Two days later a half-sister to Enable, Birdwood, was bought for 150,000gns at the Tattersalls December Mares Sale by Newsells Park Stud. The stud's general manager Julian Dollar said: 'John Gosden feels Enable might be quite useful and so do the team at Juddmonte.'

Enable continued her progress over the winter and she began her Classic season in a 1m2f conditions race at Newbury's first meeting of 2017. She faced stablemate Shutter Speed, who was also owned by Khalid Abdullah, and Gosden said he would prefer his fillies not to clash, but he was short of options.

'There's nowhere to run fillies of this nature without taking on the colts over a mile or mile and a quarter,' he said. 'They're both entitled to come on for the experience.'

Shutter Speed justified favouritism at the Berkshire track, with Frankie Dettori on board, but Enable caught the eye staying on well in to third.

RACING POST ANALYSIS – **MATT BOYLE**

Enable is a promising type but looked the second string on jockey bookings. Her impressive debut success at Newcastle in November had been boosted by the second and fourth winning on their next starts and she was solid in the market here. She looked to be going well enough three furlongs out but when switched out to challenge was unable to match the winner's pace. She was keeping on strongly to the line and shaped as though she should get further.

Enable was now prominent in the betting for the Oaks, but first she would test her credentials for the Epsom Classic in the Cheshire version. She put in an impressive performance as David Carr reported:

Enable sprints clear of Alluringly in the Cheshire Oaks to record a cosy success at Chester

Forget Frankel fever. Perhaps bloodstock experts should have been focusing on Nathaniel neurosis all along.

The 2011 King George VI and Queen Elizabeth Stakes winner came within half a length of beating the horse of the century on their debut at Newmarket in 2010 and chased him home in third place in the Champion Stakes at Ascot two years later.

But he could just make it third time lucky by beating his old rival in the race to be the first to sire a Classic winner, thanks to his daughter Enable.

The filly, home bred by Khalid Abdullah in Nathaniel's first season at stud, scored an impressive victory by a length and three-quarters in the Cheshire Oaks, showing a smart turn of foot under Frankie Dettori.

And the filly trained, like Nathaniel, by John Gosden in Newmarket is now a best-priced 8-1 for the Investec Oaks at Epsom, for which Abdullah's Shutter Speed – who beat her at Newbury last month – goes on trial in next week's Musidora Stakes at York.

Frankie Dettori makes the first of many flying dismounts from Enable in the winner's enclosure after the Cheshire Oaks

'For a stayer she showed a good turn of foot,' said Dettori. 'I thought I was on a good stayer so had better kick first, and she quickened well.'

Abdullah's racing manager Teddy Grimthorpe said: 'She handled the track well. She's quite a lengthy filly but that's the beauty of coming to these sort of races as they are educational for both the horse and the connections!'

A Classic bid is certainly on the cards. Grimthorpe said: 'The way she travels you'd be pretty confident she'd find a mile and a half to her liking.'

He added: 'Distance is going to be an issue with Shutter Speed. I'm pretty confident Enable will stay a mile and a half but there is a question mark about Shutter Speed on her pedigree, which is why she is going to York and has the option of the Prix de Diane as well.

'How lucky are we to have these sort of choices? It's a happy position to be in.'

Enable (left) keeps early leader Erica Bing in her sights as they begin the final circuit in the Cheshire Oaks

RACING POST RATINGS VIEW – **PAUL CURTIS**

Enable's Epsom Oaks odds tumbled on the back of an impressive success, albeit she enjoyed the run of the race a little more than favourite Alluringly.

She clearly has more to find to trouble Rhododendron (117), but an above-standard RPR of 110+ leaves her well placed to find further improvement at Epsom. Alluringly also improved significantly, with her RPR of 107 enough to have landed the Cheshire Oaks in the previous ten runnings.

It was a first stakes success for Enable's sire Nathaniel as Martin Stevens explained:

Sophomore sire Nathaniel was always going to come to prominence as his progeny matured and tackled longer trips, and he was represented by his first stakes winner when daughter Enable readily scored in the Listed Cheshire Oaks at Chester.

The Newsells Park Stud resident – a son of Galileo who broke his maiden at three himself before taking the King George VI and Queen Elizabeth Stakes and Eclipse – is faring well this year, with 11 winners in Europe.

Nathaniel is also the sire of four stakes-placed runners on the continent, while Ronald R won a competitive handicap at Newmarket at the weekend.

Enable – who paid a compliment to her stablemate and fellow Juddmonte homebred Shutter Speed, who she finished two places behind at Newbury on her last run – was saddled by Nathaniel's trainer John Gosden.

As is the case with any horse bred by Juddmonte, Enable has a deep pedigree.

She is out of the Sadler's Wells mare Concentric, a Listed winner in France over 1m2f, making her a half-sister to two winners including Contribution, who finished third in the Prix de Pomone over 1m4f.

Concentric is a sister to Dance Routine, a Group 2 winner over 1m4f and the dam of five-time top-level winner Flintshire, and a half-sister to stakes winners Apsis and Space Quest.

Concentric is out of Apogee, a daughter of Shirley Heights who won the Group 3 Prix du Royaumont over 1m4f, and Apogee was in turn a daughter of Bourbon Girl, an Ile De Bourbon mare who finished second to Unite in both the Epsom and Curragh Oaks in 1987.

Concentric has a two-year-old colt by Dansili named Centroid, a yearling filly by the same sire and was covered by Frankel last year.

An interesting footnote to Enable's pedigree is her close inbreeding to Sadler's Wells. Nathaniel is a paternal grandson and Concentric is a daughter, so the Chester heroine is bred 3x2 to the legendary Coolmore sire.

Gosden had taken his time with Enable and following an impressive debut performance at Newcastle she had progressed in two runs to rank as third favourite for the Oaks.

TWO

THE OAKS

Epsom, June 2, 2017

4
ENABLE
Investec

Previous spread: Enable and Frankie Dettori come home under dark skies at Epsom as they land the Oaks in June 2017

4.30 RACE 5 — *Investec Oaks (Group 1) (Fillies) (Class 1)* **ITV**
Winner £283,550 (1m 4f 6y) **1m4f**

£500,000 guaranteed **For** 3yo fillies **Weights** 9st **Entries** 16 pay £2000 **1st Forfeit** 23 pay £2000 **Confirmed** 16 **Penalty value 1st** £283,550 **2nd** £107,500 **3rd** £53,800 **4th** £26,800 **5th** £13,450 **6th** £6,750

No. (draw)	Form	Horse	Breeding	Trainer / Owner	Age Wgt	Jockey	Rating
1 (7)	75-12	**ALLURINGLY** (USA) 23 **BF**	*b f Fastnet Rock-All For Glory*	**A P O'Brien (IRE)** D Smith & Mrs J Magnier & M Tabor	3 9-0	**Seamie Heffernan**	123
2 (6)	11-3	**CORONET** 19 **BF**	*gr f Dubawi-Approach*	**John Gosden** Denford Stud	3 9-0	**Andrea Atzeni**	116
3 (4)	242-622	**DADDYS LIL DARLING** (USA) 28	*b f Scat Daddy-Miss Hot Salsa*	**Kenneth McPeek (USA)** Normandy Farm	3 9-0	**Olivier Peslier**	123
4 (9)	1-31	**ENABLE** 23	*b f Nathaniel-Concentric*	**John Gosden** K Abdullah	3 9-0	**Frankie Dettori**	124
5 (3)	41-1	**HORSEPLAY** 26	*b f Cape Cross-Mischief Making*	**Andrew Balding** Cliveden Stud	3 9-0	**Oisin Murphy**	114
6 (8)	1-2	**ISABEL DE URBINA** (IRE) 26	*b f Lope de Vega-Roscoff*	**Ralph Beckett** Merriebelle Irish Farm Limited	3 9-0	**F M Berry**	112
7 (2)	21	**NATAVIA** 13	*ch f Nathaniel-Our Queen Of Kings*	**Roger Charlton** K Abdullah	3 9-0	**Pat Smullen**	115
8 (1)	5-4222	**POCKETFULLOFDREAMS** (FR) 20	*b f Invincible Spirit-Dubai Rose*	**A P O'Brien (IRE)** M Tabor & Mrs J Magnier & D Smith & M J Joost	h 3 9-0	**Donnacha O'Brien**	110
9 (5)	21131-2	**RHODODENDRON** (IRE) 26 **BF**	*b f Galileo-Halfway To Heaven*	**A P O'Brien (IRE)** Mrs J Magnier & M Tabor & D Smith	3 9-0	**Ryan Moore**	131
10 (10)	315-1	**SOBETSU** 19	*b f Dubawi-Lake Toya*	**Charlie Appleby** Godolphin	3 9-0	**William Buick**	123

2016 (9 ran) **Minding** (4) A P O'Brien 3 9-0 10/11F Ryan Moore RPR118

BETTING FORECAST: 10-11 Rhododendron, 5 Enable, 8 Sobetsu, 10 Coronet, Natavia, 12 Horseplay, 20 Alluringly, 33 Daddys Lil Darling, Isabel de Urbina, 100 Pocketfullofdreams.

WHILE ENABLE REMAINED on course for Epsom, Shutter Speed was now being aimed at the French Oaks after she won the Musidora Stakes at York.

Teddy Grimthorpe explained the decision: 'I've always thought a mile and a quarter seems spot on for Shutter Speed.

'I think in John's mind's eye and in Prince Khalid's she would probably head for the French Oaks. And Enable is in good form, so I hope she'd head to Epsom.'

On a dramatic afternoon at Epsom Enable delivered an electric performance as Lee Mottershead reported:

In the moments leading up to the Investec Oaks the elements ensured a mighty big bang was heard across Epsom racecourse. Come the Classic itself, a new superstar of the sport made an equally big bang as Enable forged clear of odds-on favourite Rhododendron to triumph for British Flat racing's dream team.

As torrential rain poured down and racegoers fled for cover, two exquisitely bred and enormously talented fillies fought out a gripping duel down the home straight that ended in Khalid Abdullah's latest homebred champion forging clear of Rhododendron.

There can have been few wetter Oaks but also none faster, as Enable stopped the clock in a race-record time that gave Frankie Dettori his fourth success in the coveted prize, 23 years after his first, and John Gosden his second.

Enable, sent off 6-1 second favourite behind 1,000 Guineas second Rhododendron, ridden by Ryan Moore, came to Epsom via a convincing Chester defeat of the 8-11 hotpot's stablemate Alluringly.

That opponent again ran admirably in third, albeit a yawning 11 lengths behind a five-length winner whose performance established her as both a powerful stayer and a middle-distance athlete of the highest order.

The trademark flying Dettori dismount was witnessed, but during the race he had been holding tight, unlike Olivier Peslier, who bailed out from America's Daddys Lil Darling, fearful of a gruesome colli-

Enable stretches clear of Rhododendron in the home straight at Epsom to score by five lengths in the Oaks

sion with the starting stalls after she set off like a scalded cat amid thunder and lightning.

'It wasn't nice out there,' said Dettori. 'Horses get scared. You heard the bang – I got scared. When it rains so quickly the visibility becomes very bad and the reins start slipping. You try to be extra cautious and give yourself an extra yard.

'At the back of my mind I knew I had a great chance and I knew there was a question mark about Rhododendron's stamina. I knew my filly would get to the line. When I saw Ryan not moving, I thought, 'Oh God, I'm in trouble!' then once I saw the distress signals coming out from her, I knew my filly would stay right to the end.

'In the last furlong, the conditions were so bad I daren't take my hands off the reins to celebrate. I thought just get the job done and celebrate afterwards. She's put up a very good performance – and I think she'll get better and better.'

Should Enable do that, the second half of her season will be thrilling to watch, as was this Oaks, given the manner in which the winner and second locked together from the top of the home straight.

Yet inside the final furlong Rhododendron's stamina ebbed away, leaving Gosden to celebrate a special moment for his yard's King George and Eclipse hero Nathaniel, from whose first crop Enable hails.

On his debut and swansong Nathaniel was beaten by Frankel, but in the race to sire a British Classic winner, Nathaniel – or 'good old Nathaniel', as Gosden called him – has struck first.

'The first and second are two magnificent fillies who fought all the way down the straight,' said Gosden, who also saw Coronet finish fifth.

'Ryan and Frankie are good mates who knew they had the two best fillies. Ryan had told me he was very impressed with our filly when she beat him at Chester. Going over to France the other day for the Saint-Alary, he said, "Boy, she quickened and then quickened again". It isn't often Ryan compliments someone else's horse. he's quite tight with that sort of thing.'

Gosden added: 'After Chester I felt she was as good as I've had since Taghrooda. She's in that class. I said coming down today we would have to turn over a brilliant filly. I said there was a chance we might – and we have.'

Taghrooda, the heroine here in 2014, went on to claim the King George. When such a target was suggested for Enable, the man with five runners in the Derby seemed rather taken aback.

'Jeez, that would be bold,' said Gosden. 'I'll have a word with her. She'll tell me what to do. Horses always tell you if you watch and listen.

Frankie Dettori and Teddy Grimthorpe are amused in the Epsom winner's enclosure

'There are races like the Irish Oaks and King George. There are no plans, though. We'll discuss it with Prince Khalid, he has a strong opinion on everything.'

The prince's representative on the Downs, Teddy Grimthorpe, described Enable's display as 'utterly brilliant'. Indeed it was.

'That was a proper Oaks, a real Oaks,' said Gosden. 'I thought with the drama beforehand and then the flash of lightning, it was all a bit Hollywood.'

Like any great Hollywood production, it had a marvellous leading lady.

Tom Kerr was full of admiration for Enable and Rhododendron:

If the epic thunderstorm that struck Epsom in the half hour leading up to the start of the Oaks was dramatic foreshadowing of what was to come, it was perfectly apt weather, because Enable and Rhododendron served up a titanic contest in the driving rain that any budding Spielberg would have been proud of.

This was a race awash in drama. In the run-up to it the crowd was, alternately, dashing for cover and gasping in shock as great booms rattled the stands and jagged lightning bolts came firing from the blackening sky. This was, as Enable's trainer John Gosden put it, a scene straight out of Hollywood.

The movie theme continued as the field went to post as Daddys Lil Darling, the filly courageously brought over from America by Kenny McPeek to contest the Classic, was spooked by the storm and took off at terrifying pace, forcing Olivier Peslier to take drastic action as they approached the starting stalls and the fencing beyond.

Having extricated himself from his irons, Peslier pulled the ejector cord and dived from the saddle, somehow avoiding the filly's flying hooves and rolling safely to a halt. A second career as a film stuntman will surely follow. Both horse and jockey were unscathed but that will have been only minor comfort for McPeek, whose adventurousness deserved so much more than this.

Somehow the rest of the field were kept calm – an admirable feat by the Classic jockeys and stalls handlers – and as the rain came down in ever heavier torrents the Oaks was off and running, Pocketfullofdreams heading promptly to the front to set the fractions for stablemate Rhododendron, sent off odds-on favourite under Ryan Moore.

Frankie Dettori delights the Epsom crowd with a flying dismount from Enable after the Oaks

Rhododendron had been defeated when favourite in the 1,000 Guineas, her chance effectively ended after she had no luck in running, but she had a near perfect run round here and was delivered to challenge by Ryan Moore just after the three-furlong pole, coming to the front at the same moment as Enable and Frankie Dettori launched their challenge.

This was the stuff that sport is all about: two top jockeys on two fancied mounts heaving into view under rain-lashed skies, every sinew straining as the riders asked their horses to win the race, cheered on by a delirious crowd.

It looked for a moment as if the race was Rhododendron's, but it was Enable who found more. She shrugged off the challenge of Rhododendron and went clear in tremendous fashion, five lengths by the time she crossed the line. John Gosden and Frankie Dettori teamed up to win the Derby with the sensational Golden Horn two years ago and on this evidence they have a bright new star to conquer with.

Another star of the Flat was in evidence an hour earlier in the Coronation Cup. The Aidan O'Brien-trained Highland Reel is among the most seasoned of travellers and is tougher than a pub pitbull, which may have been just as well as he and his stablemates had endured the sort of nightmare travel delays that would have most of us downing gin and tonics like quinine was going out of fashion.

Highland Reel and the entire O'Brien team arrived at the track only an hour before the Coronation Cup after a refueling mishap

Frankie Dettori punches the air after winning the Oaks on Enable

on the tarmac in Ireland sent jet fuel gushing all over the plane, meaning what should have been a simple hop across the Irish Sea turned into a ten-hour slog.

Perhaps some of that jet fuel got under Highland Reel's skin because he sprung out of the stalls like a dog that's just heard the postman come through the garden gates, shooting into a lead he relinquished for only the briefest of moments.

Godolphin's Hawkbill caused the moment of worry, ranging up alongside and heading Highland Reel just before two out, but the Ballydoyle colt might mainline Stella because he has more fight than you could believe, battling back to take the lead and a sensational victory and his fifth Group 1, crossing the line only a few hours after crossing into Britain.

'I thought maybe the journey had taken its toll,' co-owner Derrick Smith said, 'but no, he wasn't having any of it. He's so tough, and imagine the team effort to keep the horse calm, it's quite something.'

It certainly was quite something and yet another winner for the mighty Galileo, whose son Nathaniel himself had his first Classic winner as a sire when Enable won.

So who else to sum up the day but the late, great Freddy Mercury: 'Thunderbolt and lightning very, very frightening me, Galileo, Galileo!'

Enable's first run in a Group 1 marked her out as a filly from the top drawer and justified her connections' faith. It was time for her first trip overseas.

3301 **INVESTEC OAKS (GROUP 1) (FILLIES)** **1m 4f 6y**
4:30 (4:33) (Class 1) 3-Y-O
£283,550 (£107,500; £53,800; £26,800; £13,450; £6,750) **Stalls** Centre

Form				RPR
1-31	**1**		**Enable**^{23} 2523 3-9-0 107 .... FrankieDettori 9 (John Gosden) *chsd ldng pair: 3rd st: rdn and clsd to ld over 2f out: sn wnt clr w runner up: forged ent fnl f: styd on strly and drew clr fnl f: readily* **6/1^{2}**	123
31-2	**2**	*5*	**Rhododendron (IRE)**^{26} 2434 3-9-0 116 .... RyanMoore 5 (A P O'Brien, Ire) *hld up in 4th: 4th st: clsd to join ldrs over 2f out: sn wnt clr w wnr: rdn over 1f out: no ex and unable to go w wnr ent fnl f: outstyd by wnr but kpt on for clr 2nd* **8/11^{1}**	115
2	**3**	*6*	**Alluringly (USA)**^{23} 2523 3-9-0 106 .... SeamieHeffernan 7 (A P O'Brien, Ire) *hld up in midfield: 6th st: rdn and hdwy to chse clr ldng pair 2f out: sn no imp and outpcd: wl hld in 3rd and plugged on same pce after* **16/1**	105
41-1	**4**	*3¾*	**Horseplay**^{26} 2436 3-9-0 100 .... OisinMurphy 3 (Andrew Balding) *t.k.h: hld up in last trio: 7th st: rdn and carried rt over 2f out: hdwy to go modest 4th 1f out: kpt on but no ch w ldrs* **14/1**	99+
11-3	**5**	*1*	**Coronet**^{19} 2665 3-9-0 103 .... AndreaAtzeni 6 (John Gosden) *sn dropped to rr and niggled along: 8th st: swtchd rt and rdn over 2f out: no ch but kpt on to pass btn rivals 1f out: wnt modest 5th ins fnl f: n.d* **12/1^{3}**	98+
1-2	**6**	*2¾*	**Isabel De Urbina (IRE)**^{26} 2436 3-9-0 98 .... FranBerry 8 (Ralph Beckett) *hld up in last trio: 9th st: sn rdn: no prog and no ch after: plugged on to pass btn rivals fnl f* **33/1**	93
5-42	**7**	*2¾*	**Pocketfullofdreams (FR)**^{20} 2613 3-9-0 99 ....(h) DonnachaO'Brien 1 (A P O'Brien, Ire) *sn led and set decent gallop: 5 l clr st: rdn and hdd over 2f out: sn btn and dropped out: wl bhd ins fnl f* **50/1**	89
15-1	**8**	*1¾*	**Sobetsu**^{19} 2665 3-9-0 113 .... WilliamBuick 10 (Charlie Appleby) *led for 1f: chsd ldr: 2nd st: sn rdn to cl: ev ch briefly over 2f out: 3rd and totally outpcd by ldng pair 2f out: wknd over 1f out* **6/1^{2}**	86
21	**9**	*7*	**Natavia**^{13} 2827 3-9-0 102 .... PatSmullen 2 (Roger Charlton) *hld up in midfield: 5th st: rdn and outpcd whn edgd rt over 2f out: bhd over 1f out* **12/1^{3}**	75

2m 34.13s (-6.67) **Going Correction** -0.05s/f (Good) **9** Ran SP% **119.3**
Speed ratings (Par 110): **113,109,105,103,102 100,98,97,93**
CSF £11.07 CT £71.45 TOTE £6.40: £2.00, £1.10, £3.90; EX 12.10 Trifecta £93.60.
Owner K Abdullah **Bred** Juddmonte Farms Ltd **Trained** Newmarket, Suffolk

RACING POST RATINGS VIEW – **PAUL CURTIS**

Enable's ultimately dominant display in a testing Oaks ranks above par with the best winners in the past ten years with a Racing Post Rating of 122. With rain getting into the ground and a strong pace from Pocketfullofdreams, the race was set up to stretch the field and lends itself to a big figure.

But even so, with five lengths back to Rhododendron and six further lengths to Alluringly, it's hard not to see this as a superior Oaks-winning performance. The fact that Enable extended Cheshire Oaks superiority over Alluringly by nine lengths underlines the merit of her display.

The outstanding Ouija Board sets the modern Oaks-winning standard with an RPR of 124. Of more recent winners, neither Light Shift nor Look Here improved on their Epsom form subsequently, while Sariska peaked at 123 in 2009 when following up in the Irish Oaks.

KPP
DETTORI

THREE

IRISH OAKS

Curragh, July 15, 2017

Previous spread: Frankie Dettori and Enable after their victory in the Irish Oaks at the Curragh in July 2017

5.55 RACE 6 — *Darley Irish Oaks (Group 1) (Fillies)* — *Winner €228,000* — **RTE2** — **1m4f**

€400,000 guaranteed **For** 3yo fillies **Weights** 9st **Penalty value 1st** €228,000 **2nd** €76,000 **3rd** €36,000 **4th** €16,000 **5th** €8,000 **6th** €4,000

75-1236 **ALLURINGLY (USA)** 23 — 3 9-0
1 (8) *b f Fastnet Rock-All For Glory* — **Wayne Lordan** (123)
A P O'Brien Derrick Smith & Mrs John Magnier & Michael Tabor

2513 **AURORA BUTTERFLY (IRE)** 17 — h1 3 9-0
2 (1) *gr f Born To Sea-Diamonaka* — **Billy Lee** (106)
W McCreery Miss Madeline Burns

8-52150 **BEAN FEASA** 24 — t3 9-0
3 (10) *b f Dubawi-Speirbhean* — **Kevin Manning** (118)
J S Bolger Godolphin

135 **BENGALA (FR)** 27 — h1 3 9-0
4 (4) *ch f Pivotal-Bright Sky* — **Declan McDonogh** ↑ (109)
John M Oxx R S Evans

11-351 **CORONET** 23 **D1** — 3 9-0
5 (9) *gr f Dubawi-Approach* — **Olivier Peslier** (121)
John Gosden (GB) Denford Stud

1-311 **ENABLE** 43 **D1** — 3 9-0
6 (6) *b f Nathaniel-Concentric* — **Frankie Dettori** ↑ (135)
John Gosden (GB) K Abdullah

2121-2 **EZIYRA (IRE)** 37 **BF C1** — h 3 9-0
7 (3) *ch f Teofilo-Eytarna* — **Pat Smullen** (122)
D K Weld H H Aga Khan

10-4046 **INTRICATELY (IRE)** 13 **C1** — 3 9-0
8 (5) *b f Fastnet Rock-Inner Realm* — **Donnacha O'Brien** (122)
Joseph Patrick O'Brien Mrs C C Regalado-Gonzalez

110 **NAUGHTY OR NICE (IRE)** 23 — 3 9-0
9 (7) *b f Fastnet Rock-Monty's Girl* — **Colin Keane** (106)
John M Oxx Newtown Anner Stud Farm Ltd

1-74522 **RAIN GODDESS (IRE)** 13 — t3 9-0
10 (2) *b f Galileo-Where* — **Seamie Heffernan** ↑ (124)
A P O'Brien Mrs John Magnier & Michael Tabor & Derrick Smith

2016 (11 ran) **Seventh Heaven** (9) A P O'Brien 3 9-0 14/1 Seamie Heffernan RPR115

BETTING FORECAST: 2-5 Enable, 6 Coronet, Rain Goddess, 14 Alluringly, 20 Naughty Or Nice, 25 Eziyra, 40 Bean Feasa, 50 Bengala, Intricately, 100 Aurora Butterfly.

THE IRISH OAKS was the logical next step for Enable and, while everything was going the right way for the Classic-winning filly, the same could not be said about her jockey.

Frankie Dettori was forced to miss Royal Ascot after breaking a bone in his shoulder at Yarmouth in the middle of June and he only returned to the saddle in the week of the Irish Oaks.

John Gosden was happy with Enable's preparation, saying: 'She's in good form. We've freshened her up since the Oaks and she's building up nicely. I've been happy enough with her and the plan was always to go to the Curragh after she won at Epsom.

'She hasn't been over-raced. She was impressive at Chester and Epsom, and she won a two-year-old race well towards the backend. We're hopeful that she's very much going in the right direction.'

Enable was only going in one direction as Tony O'Hehir reported:

Enable had hinted at Epsom last month that she is perhaps more able than any middle-distance three-year-old of either sex, and in becoming a dual Oaks winner at the Curragh the hint became a stonking great announcement.

She completed the Epsom-Curragh Classic double with another high-class performance, winning the Darley-sponsored Irish Oaks by five and a half lengths and putting Frankie Dettori back in the Group 1 spotlight just two days after his return from injury.

Dettori, winning the Irish Oaks for the fourth time and landing his ninth Irish Classic, revealed afterwards that Enable was the prime reason he had returned to action this week at all.

After a trademark flying dismount, Dettori said: 'I probably came back a week too soon but the carrot I had in front of me was too good to resist. She was the carrot and I had to come back to ride her.'

Dettori continued: 'She's very good. I think she's improved since Epsom and the turn of foot she showed to take control of the race was very impressive.

0
6

10

Previous spread: Frankie Dettori and Enable come home five and a half lengths clear of Rain Goddess in the Irish Oaks

'I was in second gear and when I asked her to go she flew. It was hands and heels from there. She's got a great cruising speed for a stayer. She's got everything.'

Dettori had won the contest previously on Lailani in 2001, Vintage Tipple in 2003 and Blue Bunting in 2011, while Enable is the 14th filly to achieve the Oaks double, and the first since Snow Fairy in 2010.

For trainer John Gosden she was a second winner of the race, after Great Heavens in 2012, and for owner Khalid Abdullah a third after Wemyss Bight in 1993 and Bolas in 1994.

Gosden said: 'Enable is an exceptional filly and Frankie gave her a beautiful ride. We might take on the colts at some stage but she has come back with a nick on the outside of her off-fore and we'll have to check that out.

'She's in the King George and Yorkshire Oaks, but we're not making any plans today.'

Further down the road is the Qatar Prix de l'Arc de Triomphe, and bookmakers now rate her the most likely three-year-old winner of Europe's most valuable contest, quoting her as second favourite behind Almanzor at no bigger than 7-1.

By completing the Classic double, Enable confirmed her prowess and a first clash with the colts and older horses was in her sights.

RACING POST RATINGS VIEW – SAM WALKER

Enable confirmed her status as queen of the fillies with an emphatic victory and connections are understandably raising their sights to taking on the colts.

As the first dual Oaks winner since Snow Fairy in 2010 – and the highest-rated winner of the Curragh version since Sariska in 2009 – she looks too good to be kept to her own sex.

The race rather fell into her lap, as she was well placed stalking the steady pace and was still swinging on the bridle when taking up the running shortly after turning into the straight. But when asked the question by winning jockey Frankie Dettori she answered and nothing got close.

The five-and-a-half-length win over Rain Goddess (112) earned her an RPR of 121, which ranks her up with the best colts around once her filly's allowance is factored in.

Things will get tougher when she enters open company and she will have to improve again to land the Prix de l'Arc de Triomphe or King George VI and Queen Elizabeth Stakes.

The last three-year-old fillies to win the Arc – Zarkava, Danedream and Treve – did so with RPRs of 128-131, while Taghrooda improved to an RPR of 125 to win the King George after her Oaks win in 2014.

4928a **DARLEY IRISH OAKS (GROUP 1) (FILLIES)** **1m 4f**
5:55 (5:56) 3-Y-O

£194,871 (£64,957; £30,769; £13,675; £6,837; £3,418)

RPR

1 **Enable**^{43} 3301 3-9-0 120 .... FrankieDettori 6 121+
(John Gosden) *settled bhd ldr in 2nd: impr gng wl to ld over 2f out where pushed along: sn rdn and qcknd clr: styd on strly to assert ins fnl f: eased cl home: easily* **2/5**^{1}

2 *5 ½* **Rain Goddess (IRE)**^{13} 4419 3-9-0 110 .... (t) SeamieHeffernan 2 112
(A P O'Brien, Ire) *on toes befhand: sn led: disp 3rd at 1/2-way: 4th into st: impr into 2nd and rdn 2f out: no imp on easy wnr u.p ent fnl f: kpt on same pce* **7/1**^{3}

3 *2* **Eziyra (IRE)**^{37} 3511 3-9-0 106 .... (h) PatSmullen 3 109
(D K Weld, Ire) *in rr of mid-div early: 7th 1/2-way: hdwy 2f out to chse ldrs: rdn in 3rd under 2f out and no imp on easy wnr ent fnl f: kpt on same pce* **20/1**

4 *1 ¼* **Coronet**^{23} 3995 3-9-0 108 .... OlivierPeslier 9 107+
(John Gosden) *hld up towards rr: racd keenly early: last at 1/2-way: pushed along in rr into st and sme hdwy on outer 2f out: wnt 4th ins fnl f and kpt on clsng stages: nvr trbld ldrs* **6/1**^{2}

5 *2 ½* **Aurora Butterfly (IRE)**^{17} 4208 3-9-0 93 .... (h^{1}) WJLee 1 103
(W McCreery, Ire) *in rr early: tk clsr order in 9th after 1f: hdwy in 8th under 3f out and impr between horses 2f out where n.m.r: rdn to dispute 4th over 1f out and sn no ex: one pce in 5th wl ins fnl f* **66/1**

6 *1 ¼* **Alluringly (USA)**^{23} 3995 3-9-0 106 .... WayneLordan 8 101
(A P O'Brien, Ire) *in rr of mid-div early: 6th 1/2-way: pushed along on outer in 6th under 3f out: sn rdn and no ex disputing 4th over 1f out: one pce after* **16/1**

7 *2* **Intricately (IRE)**^{13} 4419 3-9-0 108 .... DonnachaO'Brien 5 98
(Joseph Patrick O'Brien, Ire) *hld up in tch: 5th 1/2-way: pushed along in 5th into st: sn rdn bhd ldrs on outer and no ex between horses over 1f out: sn wknd* **20/1**

8 *5* **Bean Feasa**^{24} 3964 3-9-0 101 .... (t) KevinManning 10 90
(J S Bolger, Ire) *chsd ldrs: racd keenly early: disp 3rd at 1/2-way: pushed along in 3rd into st and sn no ex u.p: wknd 2f out* **33/1**

9 *¾* **Bengala (FR)**^{27} 3874 3-9-0 94 .... (h^{1}) DeclanMcDonogh 4 89
(John M Oxx, Ire) *broke wl to ld: over 2 l clr at 1/2-way: pressed clly into st: rdn and hdd over 2f out: wknd* **33/1**

10 *7 ½* **Naughty Or Nice (IRE)**^{23} 3995 3-9-0 99 .... ColinKeane 7 77
(John M Oxx, Ire) *w.w towards rr: niggled along briefly in 8th at 1/2-way: rdn and no imp over 2f out: wknd: eased ins fnl f* **16/1**

2m 32.13s (-6.57) **Going Correction** -0.125s/f (Firm) **10** Ran SP% **126.9**
Speed ratings: **116,112,111,110,108 107,106,103,102,97**
CSF £4.20 CT £34.79 TOTE £1.40: £1.02, £1.50, £3.30; DF 4.40 Trifecta £27.20.
Owner K Abdullah **Bred** Juddmonte Farms Ltd **Trained** Newmarket, Suffolk

FOUR

KING GEORGE VI AND QUEEN ELIZABETH STAKES

Ascot, July 29, 2017

10

Previous spread: Frankie Dettori is unable to contain his joy after Enable's first victory in the King George VI and Queen Elizabeth Stakes at Ascot in July 2017

3.35 RACE 4

King George VI And Queen Elizabeth Stakes (Sponsored By Qipco) (Group 1) (British Champions Series) (Class 1) **ITV**

Winner £652,165 (1m 3f 211y) **1m4f**

£1,150,000 guaranteed **For** 3yo+ **Weights** 3yo colts & geldings 8st 10lb; fillies 8st 7lb; 4yo+ colts & geldings 9st 7lb; fillies 9st 4lb **Weight for age** 3 from 4yo+ 11lb **Entries** 16 pay £3500 **1st Forfeit** 24 pay £4500 **Confirmed** 16 pay £2000.00 **Penalty value 1st** £652,165 **2nd** £247,250 **3rd** £123,740 **4th** £61,640 **5th** £30,935 **6th** £15,525

1 (9) 132-123 **DESERT ENCOUNTER** (IRE) 21 D2 CD1 — h 5 9-7
b g Halling-La Chicana
David Simcock Abdulla Al Mansoori — **Sean Levey** (123)

2 (4) 212-711 **HIGHLAND REEL** (IRE) 38 D4 C1 CD1 — 5 9-7
b h Galileo-Hveger
A P O'Brien (IRE) Derrick Smith & Mrs John Magnier & Michael Tabor — **Ryan Moore** (131)

3 (3) 21U5-61 **IDAHO** (IRE) 35 D1 CD1 — 4 9-7
b c Galileo-Hveger
A P O'Brien (IRE) Michael Tabor & Derrick Smith & Mrs John Magnier — **Seamie Heffernan** (127)

4 (2) 3/P3-18 **JACK HOBBS** 38 BF D3 — b 5 9-7
br h Halling-Swain's Gold
John Gosden Godolphin & Partners — **William Buick** (130)

5 (10) 50200-4 **MAVERICK WAVE** (USA) 35 — 6 9-7
ch h Elusive Quality-Misty Ocean
John Gosden Godolphin — **Graham Lee** (120)

6 (6) 554-324 **MY DREAM BOAT** (IRE) 27 C1 — p 5 9-7
b h Lord Shanakill-Betty Burke
Clive Cox Paul & Clare Rooney — **Adam Kirby** (126)

7 (8) 124-131 **ULYSSES** (IRE) 21 D1 — 4 9-7
ch c Galileo-Light Shift
Sir Michael Stoute Flaxman Stables Ireland Ltd — **Jim Crowley** (131)

8 (5) 1521-13 **SIXTIES SONG** (ARG) 65 BF D2 — 4 9-3
b c Sixties Icon-Blissful Song
Alfredo F Gaitan Dassie (ARG) Santa Elena — **Gerald Mosse** (123)

9 (1) 13251 **BENBATL** 37 C1 — t 3 8-10
b c Dubawi-Nahrain
Saeed Bin Suroor Godolphin — **Oisin Murphy** (121)

10 (7) 1-3111 **ENABLE** 14 D2 — 3 8-7
b f Nathaniel-Concentric
John Gosden K Abdullah — **Frankie Dettori** (131)

2016 (7 ran) **Highland Reel** (3) A P O'Brien 4 9-7 13/8F — Ryan Moore RPR121

BETTING FORECAST: 5-4 Enable, 9-2 Highland Reel, Jack Hobbs, 8 Ulysses, 10 Idaho, 16 Benbatl, 25 Desert Encounter, My Dream Boat, 66 Sixties Song, 200 Maverick Wave.

FOLLOWING THE IRISH OAKS Teddy Grimthorpe suggested that Enable might wait until the Yorkshire Oaks rather than run next in the King George VI and Queen Elizabeth Stakes.

'At this point it's more likely she'll head to the Yorkshire Oaks next and, as chairman of York racecourse, I'm most pleased about it, although it wasn't my decision!' he said.

Looking further ahead, Grimthorpe added: 'We'll take it a race at a time with Enable and all decisions about targets and whether she stays in training will be made later on.'

Enable was the apple of Frankie Dettori's eye and had played a huge part in the Italian superstar's recent renaissance. He spoke to Lee Mottershead about his return to the top:

The most famous jockey in the world arrives at an upmarket London hotel in the shadow of St Paul's Cathedral ready to talk and with plenty to talk about. He may be in pain but the discomfort has been eased by a second Classic success aboard his latest four-legged superstar. For Frankie Dettori, three decades on from his first British winner, there continues to be much in the way of both fame and glory.

He is immaculately dressed in a crisp, slim-fit black suit and stylish crimson tie. These are the sartorial standards one imagines Dettori invariably maintains when in the capital, to which he has headed not only to give the umpteenth Racing Post interview of his career but also to promote the Qatar Goodwood Festival, a meeting whose sponsorship is linked closely to one of his two main employers, Sheikh Joaan Al Thani.

Dettori is a fan of those five days on the Sussex Downs but an even bigger fan of the biggest five days of all.

This time the 46-year-old father-of-five missed Royal Ascot after sustaining a fracture to his left shoulder in a Yarmouth paddock accident exactly seven days before Flat racing's most prestigious fixture was due to begin. With Dettori present only in the form of the statue created following his 1996 Magnificent Seven, Lady Aurelia,

Frankie Dettori shows his affection for Enable after the Irish Oaks, with groom Imran Shahwani looking on

Big Orange, Coronet and Stradivarius all won races under someone other than their intended partner.

'You got the questions, I got the answers,' are the first words spoken by Dettori, who had briefly interrupted his spell on the sidelines to ride Shutter Speed into fourth in the Prix de Diane. His experience at Chantilly was not a happy one, so much so he did not ride competitively again until the Thursday of Newmarket's July festival, where he began to warm up for what proved to be a resounding Irish Oaks success on Enable, as dominant at the Curragh as she had been at Epsom.

By the time Enable preps for the Prix de l'Arc de Triomphe, almost certainly in the Darley Yorkshire Oaks, Dettori should once again be as good as new. For now, though, he remains what he calls 'a work in progress', his body still recovering from that seaside spill.

'I thought I heard a little crack,' says Dettori, recalling the fall. 'Straightaway I started lying to myself that I was all right. I was hoping maybe I'd just sprained it. Then I started thinking: 'Dear God, I've only got one week until Ascot and only five days until Shutter Speed'.

'I chose not to have it X-rayed at that stage as I was scared in case it showed the shoulder was broken. I kept telling myself: 'I'm all right, I'm all right'. I wasn't all right. I couldn't lift my arm. I couldn't touch my nose.

'On the Sunday I strapped myself up and took painkillers. My thinking was I only had to ride in one race and I thought the filly would go round on the bridle. She nearly did, but when Senga came and we got into a battle, I had to really push. It was then I knew I had broken it.

'There were 20 seconds of intense pain when I was pushing her to the line. I was in agony. I couldn't even put my socks on afterwards. I realised then I was in a terrible mess.'

It was only on Ascot's opening morning that Dettori announced his own scratching. He had known, however, the day before.

'After resting the arm overnight it felt a bit better on the Monday morning,' he says. 'I went to the hospital and had an X-ray. The guy told me: "You're not going to Ascot." At that point I had to accept the truth.

'I was devastated but what could I do? I stayed at home for the first day and watched Lady Aurelia win. Then I told my wife I was going home to Italy. "Come with me," I said. "I can't," she said. "I've got the kids." So I got on a plane and left.

'I still watched every race but I was with my parents in a different environment. I didn't have to face people saying: 'Bad luck, bad luck.' Obviously I was sad, but I was also as relaxed as I could have been in the circumstances.

'I wanted the horses to win and I cheered them all home. These are horses I knew I'd be riding in the future. I put a lot of work into Lady Aurelia last year. She has become close to me. Big Orange's owners, Bill and Tim Gredley, are very good friends of mine as I was their neighbour for 18 years. I work for John, so I obviously wanted his horses to do well. I spoke to most of the people who were riding my horses, too. That way I still felt a little bit part of it.'

Yet a bit part is all he was. For his triumphant return, the sport had to wait for the latest chapter in the story of Enable, a filly trained by John Gosden, who resuscitated Dettori's career following the messy Godolphin divorce. In steering Khalid Abdullah's homebred to a five-and-a-half-length triumph, it became wonderfully clear to Dettori that, only two years on from Golden Horn, he is once again associated with a superstar.

'She was my inspiration to come back – I moved mountains to get there,' he admits.

'I was very confident but still surprised by how she won. I knew she was good but she really gave me the wow factor. Only very few horses do that. You get the odd moment like when Golden Horn took off in the Arc. Very few horses ever take off like he did that day, but she took off at the Curragh.

'Both visually and from the feeling she gives you from the saddle, she is very good. She hasn't been tested or challenged by any colts yet. She hasn't faced older horses, either. They will be the big tests – but I'm confident she can match up to the very best around.

'The Arc is something John and I have talked about quietly for a while. We knew she had the potential to be a very interesting Arc contender but she had to put up a performance like she did in the Irish Oaks to get herself in the picture. Her cruising speed, acceleration and stamina make you think she has everything you need to be competitive in the Arc.'

That may be so, but back in April, when Enable and Shutter Speed met in a Newbury conditions race, the future dual Classic heroine – discarded on that occasion by Dettori – could manage only third.

'Shutter Speed is a more exuberant worker,' he explains. 'Enable goes through the motions in the morning. In the afternoon she turns into a monster. She becomes a different horse. In the mornings she is very quiet and doesn't get your blood pumping. That's why she started out at Newbury this season as the second string.

'After Newbury we went to the trial at Chester and even I was surprised. My thinking was she was one-paced, so I'd have to kick early, but she delivered a turn of foot I wasn't expecting. That told us she was special. Then she won the Oaks, although even at Epsom when Rhododendron came beside me, I thought: "Oh God. This is going to be a struggle." I was wrong. She found another gear. That's three times now she has shown she is up there with the best.'

Dettori has shown himself to be up with the best for approaching three decades. The first Group 1 win came in 1990, three years after he broke his British duck as a teenager who not so long earlier had been hopelessly homesick and keen to return to Sardinia, from where his father (and former top jockey), Gianfranco, had sent him aged 14. That initial victory in his adopted homeland came at Goodwood, where he is set to be reunited with Gold Cup hero Big Orange.

'It's going to be beautiful,' says Dettori. 'Big Orange wears his heart on his sleeve. It took me a while to work him out, but I was the one who pushed for him to run in the Gold Cup. He has won the Goodwood Cup twice but with him the key is we need Glorious to be glorious. We don't want too much rain.

'He is an exciting horse to ride. Like Persian Punch, Double Trigger and Yeats, he is a stayer who has caught the racing public's imagination. He has a likeable name as well.

'I'm looking forward to the whole meeting. As a festival it has grown massively in stature in recent years thanks to the Qatar sponsorship and the injection of prize-money. I've been very successful over those five days, but the truth is Goodwood either loves you or hates you. One day you can go there with five chances but all of them are drawn wide. That can ruin five chances.'

Win or lose, there will be many punters who will back Dettori's horses simply because Dettori is riding them. The face of racing is indisputably Frankie. His name will be recognised by almost any man or woman on the street and they will be able to tell you what he does. That would surely be true of no other current jockey. Indeed, such is the huge chasm in public (and wider media) popularity between Dettori and the rest, some fear for the Flat once Dettori chooses to sign off.

'I've been very lucky,' he insists. 'I've been around for 30 years, although I've only been really famous since 1996 when I won the seven races at Ascot. That's what made me a household name. I've been on a pedestal for the last 21 years because of that.

'I've also been in the limelight because I survived a plane crash that was worldwide news. I've had my achievements but also my troubles and the controversial crap. Of course I am where I am partly because of things that have been my doing but also because of circumstances.

'I did everything, *Top of the Pops*, *A Question of Sport*, *Big Brother*, the whole lot, but I'm a personality who likes all that. I have no malice or blame towards any of my colleagues for not being me.

'When I'm not there I think there will be someone else. Before me there was Willie Carson. Racing is an entertainment sport and it's very much in the public eye, so there will always be someone, but at the moment, perhaps because I've been around for so long, I overshadow most of the others. At some point, though, when I'm not there someone else will take the baton.'

For now, and in all probability for a few years to come given he plans to ride beyond his 50th birthday, the baton remains in Dettori's hands. As we sit on a sofa, other journalists edge closer, keen for their appointed time with a celebrity who in recent weeks has been interviewed not only by racing hacks but also by ITV's *Loose Women* and on the BBC's *The One Show*, on whose sofa he was joined by son Rocco.

'He wants to be a jockey but he's only 12 and they change their mind every five minutes at that age,' says Dettori, who initially gives a negative answer when asked if he would like Rocco to follow in his father's footsteps by becoming a jockey.

'Not really, no,' he says. 'He's my son and it's dangerous. If you don't succeed he will find it's 30 years of struggle. On the other hand, I would be very proud as he would be the third generation. If he does make it he'll have a great life, an absolutely smashing life.'

For the second generation, life is perhaps most bella when back home. Sant'Anna Arresi in South Sardinia was his hiding place for the final four days of the royal meeting. Had he been at Ascot he would have been stopped wherever he went. Not so in his little Italian safe haven.

'No-one really knows me there apart from my parents and my mates,' says Dettori.

'Everyone else might recognise my name through seeing it in newspapers but they wouldn't know what I look like. That's great. I feel really at ease and relaxed there. It's a small town with maybe 1,500 to 2,000 people, about three miles from the beach. I can wear my shorts and flip-flops and just be Joe Bloggs.

'When I'm there my dad is always on my case, saying I should have done this, should have done that, but that's only because he was a jockey and he wants what's best for me.

'My mum is the one who spoils me. She cooks all her best dishes when I'm home. I'm so spoiled that I even make my own menu. In the morning I say to her I'd like suckling pig for dinner, or I might go for lamb, pasta or lobster. Then off she goes shopping, she prepares food for me throughout the day and then I come back from the beach and my dinner is there waiting for me. Beautiful!'

Fast forward 20 years, can Rocco expect the same treatment if returning home to see his folks as a world-famous jockey? 'No way,' says Dettori. 'He can go feed himself!'

Dettori's insight into Enable revealed just how much she had impressed him and it was no surprise that Gosden was now considering a crack at the King George.

He said: 'Enable cantered this morning and seems fine in herself and, as she flew to Ireland and back, she didn't take that much out of herself.

'As the Yorkshire Oaks is that much later this year it makes sense to have a look at Ascot while she's in such good form.'

Gosden was unconcerned about the quick turnaround from the Irish Classic. 'We think two weeks [from the Curragh to Ascot] will be enough as long as we're happy with her, although everything has to be confirmed with the owner,' he said. 'She's progressive and has done nothing but improve through her races.'

The weight-for-age conditions in the King George favoured Enable, but it meant that Dettori had to win a battle with the scales to make the weight.

Dettori made the weight and Enable put up a stunning performance as Jon Lees reported:

Enable was a stone apart on the racecard and proved a class apart on the racecourse as she joined an illustrious group of great fillies to win the King George VI and Queen Elizabeth Stakes.

John Gosden hailed her the best filly he has trained after the Oaks and Irish Oaks winner produced another dominant victory that propelled her into the superstar bracket.

Not one of the year's Derby winners turned up for the clash of the generations, but Enable might well have beaten them anyway in showing she could well be head and shoulders above the rest of her age group in the course of a four-and-a-half length win in the Qipco-sponsored feature.

Being run in a downpour – although not as torrential as when Enable had scored at Epsom – the race did not provide the conditions in which last year's winner Highland Reel could mount much of a defence.

But even his best might not have been good enough as Enable, receiving 14lb in fillies and weight-for-age allowance, coasted past him on the bend and quickened clear for an impressive success that propelled her to a best-priced 9-4 (from 9-2) with Betfair for the Qatar Prix de l'Arc de Triomphe.

Eclipse winner Ulysses was briefly cruising on her heels, but once Frankie Dettori let her go second place was the best that could be expected for the Sir Michael Stoute representative.

QIPC
ENABLE

Previous spread: Frankie Dettori waves his whip in celebration as Enable runs away with the King George at Ascot

Idaho ran on for third, with his big brother and Aidan O'Brien-trained stablemate Highland Reel fourth.

In landing Ascot's midsummer showpiece, Enable matched some of the sport's best known fillies such as Park Top, Dahlia, Pawneese, Time Charter, Danedream and Taghrooda – another Oaks and King George winner from the Gosden stable.

'She's a wonderful filly,' said Gosden. 'To follow in the likes of Dahlia and Pawneese and even Taghrooda says a lot.

'I noticed Aidan's horses were staying wide, looking for the better ground and what they didn't race on yesterday, and they were all front rank together. Frankie knew she stayed, was on a good filly and didn't want to take back and get in trouble. She exploded early in the straight. Ulysses made a wonderful run at her but she's a very smart filly and understandably gets weight as a three-year-old against her elders.

A trademark flying dismount from Frankie Dettori in the winner's enclosure

'The King George has always been a meeting of the generations and I've always been keen on it, as I was with Nathaniel and Taghrooda. Last year Wings Of Desire was second to an older horse.

'She'd have won on good ground. She can handle anything. She's won on Tapeta, good to firm and now soft to loose.'

Gosden was winning his third King George in seven years, the first with Enable's sire Nathaniel. Taghrooda went on to contest the Yorkshire Oaks and Arc, finishing second and third, and Enable is set to follow the same path.

'I think she's the best filly I've trained,' continued Gosden. 'Royal Heroine in America, Taghrooda and her are fabulous fillies. Then there's The Fugue and Dar Re Mi. I love great fillies to train. They're a pleasure to be around.

Enable and Frankie Dettori are congratulated after winning the King George

'The style of her winning makes her great – it's quite obvious she wants to race. She just wants things to go her way and takes the race by the horns.'

He added: 'The plan has very much been the Yorkshire Oaks. This popped up in between. York's now where we want to go, and then freshen up and see where we are in terms of the Arc.'

Gosden praised the dedication of Dettori, who after fracturing a shoulder last month fought his way back to fitness and dieted in order to ride at 8st 7lb.

'The days of not eating have paid off,' said Dettori. 'I could do with a good burger now.

'She goes on any ground and now she has proved she can match up with older horses, which is what I thought. She's very good.

'The doctor said it would take three months to return and I came back in five weeks. A horse like this is the key. You need something to push you, and she's worth it.'

Dettori said that getting down to 8st 7lb was worth the effort:

When John [Gosden] rang me on Sunday and said Enable was going to run in the King George I didn't know if I wanted to be happy or cry. I was happy because it's a million-pound race but I also knew I had to lose 7lb.

I lost 7lb in six days. I had water and fish for a week, which is boring, but I wouldn't let anybody else ride her.

She's a superstar. I told John I've not had a feeling like that since Golden Horn won the Arc. I knew she was up to the task but I didn't expect her to do that. She destroyed them. She is uncomplicated, has a good mind, all the things you want.

I was confident and then this morning when I started reading the negative things like she might not like the ground I thought, well, if they've got to give a stone to a superstar that's a big task for them.

If she turned up like she usually does I knew she'd be very hard to beat, and she proved that. I was a bit worried about being stuck a bit wide drawn seven, so I thought, 'We have a stall advantage, let's get her forward, let them play catch-up with me'.

I took it up round the bend and heard the commentator say I was clear, and I was able to enjoy it.

I'm now most looking forward to a glass of champagne – the eating can come later.

John Gosden watches on as Enable goes to post for the King George

I had a week to do it so I had plenty of time to pace myself. I stuck to a strict regime and it was worth it. She's a filly for the Arc.

Lee Mottershead was full of praise for another great run:

The rain poured down and we all got soaked but it mattered not one jot, for at Ascot this King George day we were in the presence of greatness.

A great filly ridden by a great jockey and prepared by a great trainer won what, in many ways, has always been British Flat racing's greatest contest.

The sport's midsummer showpiece is not quite what it once was, simply because the sport itself has changed so dramatically, yet Enable ensured this was a Qipco-backed King George VI and Queen Elizabeth Stakes that can justifiably be compared to some of its finest runnings.

The very fact Enable was sent off at 5-4 underlined the impression she had made in claiming Classics at Epsom and the Curragh.

At both venues she posted wide-margin successes under Frankie Dettori, but the second of those wins came just two weeks ago. Her presence in Ireland led many of us to believe connections had already decided against sending the daughter of Nathaniel – a King George winner just six years ago – to Ascot. We were wrong in that assumption. Wonderfully wrong.

Enable wins the King George with her ears pricked

John Gosden trained Nathaniel. He also trained Taghrooda, who in 2014 converted Oaks success into King George glory. He now trains Enable and was quick to confirm this is the most talented filly ever to enter his care.

She must also now be of at least similar standing to Golden Horn, who two years ago triumphed for the trainer and his born again jockey in the Prix de l'Arc de Triomphe, to which she herself will head, via the Knavesmire next month.

Given Taghrooda was turned over there as a 1-5 hotpot, there could be some anxious moments when she enters York's starting stalls. If, however, she turns up in anything approaching peak form she will saunter through the Darley Yorkshire Oaks. She will then head to Chantilly, where Almanzor and Brametot will need to be exceptionally good to beat her.

The field that sought to do the same here was far from shoddy. Indeed, this was a deep King George, and even if Highland Reel and Jack Hobbs were below par, the excellent runner-up Ulysses was not.

When Sir Michael Stoute talks about the Coral-Eclipse hero he does so with a sense of complete belief in the colt's ability. It is absolutely clear he rates Ulysses highly and there was no indication he felt any disappointment in his stable star's latest display. This was simply a case of a very good boy being floored by an outstanding girl.

That girl raced keenly in the early stages and did so while being the one to race closest to a pacemaker who set fractions that were not pedestrian. Neither factor prevented her from storming clear once Dettori set her alight early in the straight.

The plaudits she received were merited. So, too, were those dished out to Dettori.

Frankie is a showman, a celebrity, an entertainer. First and foremost, though, he is a jockey. Moreover, he is a hugely professional jockey. He rushed back from a fractured shoulder to make the Irish Oaks. To make Ascot he spent the week living on white fish and water. Frankie makes us smile. He should also have us nodding our heads in approval and admiration.

'He rode her when he wasn't 100 per cent in Ireland and he has got himself here today,' said Gosden.

'He has killed himself to do this weight. His hunger and passion for the game are undimmed – and I find that quite remarkable.'

There were also words of praise for 46-year-old Dettori, and indeed for Gosden, from a man absent from Ascot for 31 years.

Khalid Abdullah has not been a regular presence on Britain's racecourses since the Frankel era closed. Nor is he a young man. The sport will be immeasurably better if the bloodstock operation he created can continue to flourish for years to come.

As such, the presence at Ascot of his son Prince Ahmed Bin Khalid was very much to be welcomed – as was the delight he plainly took from his visit.

'I promised my father I would bring the trophy back,' the Prince said. 'I told John, "Please don't make a liar out of me". I'm grateful to Frankie and John that they didn't make a liar out of me.

'The last time I was at Ascot was 1986 when Dancing Brave won. I was at college in America, so with my grey hairs now you know how old I am!

'That was my first King George, and that was Dancing Brave, but this filly was very, very impressive.

'She's lovely. She comes very close to our male horses. I think this is the best filly we've ever owned.'

Asked if he loves racing in the same way his father does, he added: 'We all do, but we always take a back stage. He's our leader. He's watching on television right now. I'm very happy for him.'

Those who got soaked watching Enable win the King George will have gone home very happy as well.

Lee Mottershead offered further thoughts on the King George the following day:

In a supremely high-class sign-off to ITV's Saturday Ascot coverage, one indeed of which the mighty Desmond Lynam would have been proud, Ed Chamberlin closed with the words: 'King George day belonged to one horse – she was ready, willing, Enable.'

Very able, in fact. There is always a danger that comes with the powerful influence of immediacy. In the heat of the moment, enthused by a stunning display in the way a sports fan should be, we can get a tad carried away by a performance, immersing ourselves in the here and now and failing to contextualise what we just witnessed against what has gone before.

This time, however, it would have seemed churlish to be anything other than blown away by the manner in which Enable destroyed the high-quality field assembled against her in the King George VI and Queen Elizabeth Stakes.

It is true not all the star names who took on the challenge performed to their very best.

Even so, my belief is that Ulysses is an extremely classy thoroughbred, one riding an impressive upward curve. The manner in which he cruised into an attacking position at Sandown, and again here, was thrilling. That Enable could run right away from him to score with daylight to spare, just as she had at Epsom and the Curragh, marks her out as one of the great fillies of the modern era.

She was, of course, carrying less weight than any other runner in the contest. Due to the weight-for-age system and sex allowance, Enable covered the King George course with a full stone less on her back than Ulysses, much less than would have been the case in a comparable American Grade 1. There has been, and will continue to be, fascinating debate about whether the 11lb three-year-olds receive from four-year-olds at this time of year is excessive. There should, however, be a point on which agreement is easier to find.

Frankie Dettori celebrates after landing the King George on Enable

The defence for the current system is three-year-olds have, at this point of their careers, still to reach full maturity relative to older horses. The logical extension of that theory is surely that at the age of three a thoroughbred cannot possibly have reached his or her peak. It must therefore also be logical to say any star thoroughbred retired without injury as a three-year-old (or, heavens forbid, as a juvenile) has been removed from racing prematurely.

It has been observed in this column before that almost as annoying as the retirement of a top-class horse at three is when an owner or trainer argues that horse no longer had anything to prove. Such a comment is complete balderdash.

A still not fully mature Enable dazzled in receipt of considerable weight from older opponents. The hope now is that next year we get to see her similarly magnificent when, with roles reversed, she must concede weight to younger, less mature, rivals.

Based on what she did here, that would be a prospect to savour. As was the case with Frankel, Khalid Abdullah is showing a real relish to let Enable compete. Her presence in the King George was of huge importance to the race. Her presence in races to come, this year and hopefully beyond, will make Flat racing all the better.

Enable's King George triumph marked her out as something special and a tilt at the Prix de l'Arc de Triomphe was very much under consideration.

RACING POST RATINGS VIEW – **SAM WALKER**

Enable's four-and-a-half-length win over Ulysses was the best performance we've seen in Europe this year according to Racing Post Ratings.

After victories in the Oaks and Irish Oaks she had looked head and shoulders the best filly in training, but at Ascot she proved just as dominant against the older generation.

The dazzling success saw her peak RPR improve from 121 to 128, which makes her the leading horse in Europe this season and moves her clear at the head of the market for the Prix de l'Arc de Triomphe at a general 2-1. She was supremely impressive, seeing off Highland Reel, Jack Hobbs and Ulysses in quick succession before storming away for a decisive victory.

This success ranks her among the better recent King George winners and places her among the top ten fillies or mares worldwide since 2000 on RPRs.

Having proved she handles a softer surface, the Arc is an obvious aim, although King George/Arc winners are rarer than you might expect, with only Dylan Thomas pulling off the double in the same season in the last 20 years.

Montjeu, Hurricane Run and Danedream achieved the reverse double by winning at Ascot the year after they won the Arc.

The Arc question for Enable is not whether she has the ability, but whether she can peak again in October after winning three major races in the summer.

5394 **KING GEORGE VI AND QUEEN ELIZABETH STKS (SPONSORED BY QIPCO) (GROUP 1) (BRITISH CHAMPIONS SERIES)** **1m 3f 211y**

3:35 (3:39) (Cla£652,155 (£247,250; £123,740; £61,640; £30,935; £15,525) **Stalls** Low

3111 **1** **Enable**[14] 4928 3-8-7 122 .... FrankieDettori 7 128
(John Gosden) *t.k.h: trckd ldr: clsd to ld wl over 2f out: sn qcknd clr: shkn up over 1f out and r.o strly: impressive* **5/4**[1]

-131 **2** *4 1/2* **Ulysses (IRE)**[21] 4638 4-9-7 121 .... JimCrowley 8 123
(Sir Michael Stoute) *hld up in rr: smooth prog over 3f out to trck wnr over 2f out: sn unable to live w her but clr of rest: hld on to 2nd nr fin* **9/1**

5-61 **3** *3/4* **Idaho (IRE)**[35] 4070 4-9-7 118 .... SeamieHeffernan 3 122
(A P O'Brien, Ire) *swtg: trckd ldrs: rdn and lost pl over 3f out: prog again over 2f out: chsd clr ldng pair over 1f out: styd on* **8/1**

-011 **4** *4* **Highland Reel (IRE)**[38] 3962 5-9-7 123 .... RyanMoore 4 116
(A P O'Brien, Ire) *swtg: racd wd: prom: rdn 3f out: sn outpcd and btn: plugged on bravely fr over 1f out* **9/2**[2]

3251 **5** *2 1/4* **Benbatl**[37] 3994 3-8-10 114 .... (t) OisinMurphy 1 113
(Saeed bin Suroor) *hld up in midfield: prog over 3f out: rdn and no imp on ldrs over 2f out: wknd steadily* **14/1**

-123 **6** *6* **Desert Encounter (IRE)**[21] 4638 5-9-7 114 .... (h) SeanLevey 9 102
(David Simcock) *lw: t.k.h: hld up in rr: rdn and lft bhd fr 3f out: tk remote 6th u.p 1f out and all out to hold that pl nr fin* **33/1**

-324 **7** *shd* **My Dream Boat (IRE)**[27] 4423 5-9-7 114 .... (p) AdamKirby 6 102
(Clive Cox) *t.k.h early: hld up towards rr: drvn and no prog 3f out: wl btn after: plugged on ins fnl f and nrly snatched remote 6th* **16/1**

00-4 **8** *2* **Maverick Wave (USA)**[35] 4069 6-9-7 102 .... GrahamLee 10 99
(John Gosden) *led: clr after 3f: hdd & wknd wl over 2f out* **100/1**

3-10 **9** *11* **Jack Hobbs**[38] 3962 5-9-7 123 .... (b) WilliamBuick 2 81
(John Gosden) *trckd ldrs: prog to chal and w wnr wl over 2f out: wnt out like a light sn after: virtually p.u fnl f* **11/2**[3]

10 *4 1/2* **Sixties Song (ARG)**[65] 4-9-3 119 .... GeraldMosse 5 70
(Alfredo F Gaitan Dassie, Argentina) *w'like: t.k.h early: hld up in last pair: wknd 3f out: t.o* **33/1**

2m 36.22s (3.62) **Going Correction** +0.90s/f (Soft)
WFA 3 from 4yo+ 11lb **10** Ran SP% **118.5**
Speed ratings (Par 117): **123,120,119,116,115 111,111,109,102,99**
CSF £13.98 CT £68.43 TOTE £2.10: £1.30, £2.70, £2.10; EX 14.70 Trifecta £71.10.
Owner K Abdullah **Bred** Juddmonte Farms Ltd **Trained** Newmarket, Suffolk

FIVE

YORKSHIRE OAKS

York, August 24, 2017

Previous spread: Enable claims a fourth successive Group 1 success under Frankie Dettori in the Yorkshire Oaks at York in August 2017

3.35 RACE 4 — *Darley Yorkshire Oaks (Group 1) (British Champions Series) (Fillies & Mares) (Class 1)* **ITV**

Winner £198,485 (1m 3f 188y) **1m4f**

£350,000 guaranteed **For** 3yo+ fillies & mares **Weights** 3yo 8st 12lb; 4yo+ 9st 7lb **Weight for age** 3 from 4yo 9lb **Entries** 9 pay £1525 **1st Forfeit** 23 pay £1750 **2nd Forfeit** 9 pay £1100 **Confirmed** 9 **Penalty value 1st** £198,485 **2nd** £75,250 **3rd** £37,660 **4th** £18,760 **5th** £9,415 **6th** £4,725

215-123 **ABINGDON** (USA) 18 **BF D1 CD1** — 4 9-7
1 *b f Street Cry-Justlookdontouch* — **Richard Kingscote**
(3) **Sir Michael Stoute** Ballymacoll Stud — (119)

1527-11 **NEZWAAH** 53 — 4 9-7
2 *b f Dubawi-Ferdoos* — **Andrea Atzeni**
(4) **Roger Varian** Sheikh Ahmed Al Maktoum — (124)

331-446 **QUEEN'S TRUST** 21 — 4 9-7
3 *b f Dansili-Queen's Best* — **Jim Crowley**
(2) **Sir Michael Stoute** Cheveley Park Stud — (122)

-123661 **ALLURINGLY** (USA) 8 — 3 8-12
4 *b f Fastnet Rock-All For Glory* — **Ryan Moore**
(5) **A P O'Brien (IRE)** Derrick Smith et al — (117)

11-3514 **CORONET** 40 **D1** — 3 8-12
5 *gr f Dubawi-Approach* — **Olivier Peslier**
(6) **John Gosden** Denford Stud — (115)

1-31111 **ENABLE** 26 **D3** — 3 8-12
6 *b f Nathaniel-Concentric* — **Frankie Dettori**
(1) **John Gosden** K Abdullah — (134)

2016 (12 ran) **Seventh Heaven** (10) A P O'Brien 3 8-11 100/30 Colm O'Donoghue RPR121

BETTING FORECAST: 1-3 Enable, 7 Nezwaah, 9 Queen's Trust, 16 Alluringly, Coronet, 25 Abingdon.

ENABLE'S POSITION AT the head of the betting for the Prix de l'Arc de Triomphe was strengthened in the middle of August when her two main market rivals, Almanzor and Brametot, disappointed at Deauville.

Before Longchamp, though, Enable would have to negotiate the Yorkshire Oaks. She put in a stellar display on the Knavesmire as Jon Lees reported:

Enable has been pulling up trees all year and Khalid Abdullah's superstar filly continued her impressive march towards the Qatar Prix de l'Arc de Triomphe when she claimed her fourth Oaks at York.

With the Cheshire Oaks, the Oaks, Irish Oaks, plus the considerable prize of the King George VI and Queen Elizabeth Stakes already secured there was more to lose than gain in contesting Yorkshire's version at odds of 1-4. But even on a track that has proved a graveyard for the likes of Sariska, Snow Fairy, Was and trainer John Gosden's other King George-winning filly Taghrooda, nothing could stop Enable's ascent to greatness.

In part a dress rehearsal for her Chantilly challenge in October, Frankie Dettori put her front-running prowess to the test. She passed with flying colours, quickening three furlongs out and needing just hands and heels to score by five lengths.

'She pricked her ears and did it well, and Frankie said she got lonely in the last part,' said Gosden.

'She needed something to come to her and make her go and he said she was looking around and idling, but I don't mind as she was well clear. It was not her favourite way of racing but she can do it that way.

'We had an awful lot to lose. Remember I was here with Taghrooda, so I know the feeling.

'In the last two furlongs she was plain bored and wanted a bit of company, but she has won by five lengths and she can't do more than that.

'It was lovely to come here for a Group 1 of this quality and let her race. It was a lovely prep for the Arc. We will let her down a bit, but

Enable and Frankie Dettori finish in splendid isolation in the Yorkshire Oaks

we have to keep cantering her as she gets very fresh and then just build her up to the Arc.'

Enable is a top-priced evens, from 5-4, to extend her streak at Chantilly in the Arc.

'That's a bit silly, but we'll give it a go,' Gosden said.

'She would be the best mile-and-a-half filly I have ever trained. Golden Horn would be the best mile-and-a-half colt. The Fugue was best at a mile and a quarter and Royal Heroine was best at a mile.

'If there was no pace you wouldn't be frightened of making all there. That was one thing I wanted, to let her use her stride today to find that out. Chantilly is a tricky track because they go fast and take a pull on the bend.'

Enable illuminated the Knavesmire just five years after Frankel was the headline act in the Juddmonte International and Abdullah's racing manager Teddy Grimthorpe, also the racecourse chairman, recognised there would be a clamour to see her return next year.

'I know there is a great desire to see the good horses go on and on and she had a fairly limited two-year-old career,' he said.

'We have to see how she is and see what the plan of attack would be again – the most important thing is her wellbeing.

Frankie Dettori acknowledges the crowd as he returns to the York winner's enclosure on Enable

'We understand it is an important thing for racing to have a filly of this calibre because she is a big attraction.

'We will take that into consideration, but the number-one priority is how she comes out of her races and what primarily Prince Khalid would like to do.'

The battle for the places was also won by Gosden as Coronet caught Queen's Trust to seal second place.

Dettori revelled in another sensational display from Enable:

She is easy for me to ride. She has a great temperament, she has unbelievable stamina, she is a stayer with a turn of foot and she is uncomplicated.

I would prefer to have a lead, but she is sensible enough to make the running and that's another option we have in the Arc and it's a small field – we've got that weapon in our armoury.

If you try to keep up with her, she'll break your lungs.

I know she won by five lengths but she had some left, believe it or not. I've felt every time I've ridden her, when something comes to her she gets going.

Frankie Dettori gives the York racegoers an opportunity to salute Enable after her Yorkshire Oaks victory

Today she was by herself but she has still won by five lengths. I said to John [Gosden] that if something sniffed her backside she would have taken off but she was far too clever.

She was floating but her floating was five lengths better than the rest! I'm as impressed with her as you guys, winning four Group 1s by five lengths.

I said to John after the Irish Oaks that I hadn't had a feel like it since Golden Horn in the Arc. She is top-drawer and keeps delivering.

Is she the best filly I've ever ridden? She could be, but she's got to win an Arc.

She is entitled to be favourite for the Arc and we've got five weeks of sleepless nights before then! We just want to get her there in the same shape.

Lee Mottershead witnessed another imperious performance:

She had more to lose than to gain, much more, in fact, so it was with a sense of trepidation many will have awaited and then watched the Yorkshire Oaks.

For folk to worry about a horse in which they have not a penny of financial investment, that horse needs to mean something. Enable very definitely means something.

Without wishing to question the judgement of John Gosden, some of us half wondered why she was here.

Enable entered the stalls of the Ebor festival's day two feature having won an Oaks, Irish Oaks and then, topping both those Classics, the King George VI and Queen Elizabeth Stakes.

She was already odds-on favourite in places for the Prix de l'Arc de Triomphe. By the time the final chapter in her racing story is penned, there was seldom any chance a Darley Yorkshire Oaks success would get much of a mention.

Yet Enable is a racehorse and racehorses are meant to race. The sport works better that way. She is also a British-based racehorse and it was much better for British racing that the fourth highest-rated racehorse in the world prepped for the Arc here on the Knavesmire than at Chantilly in the Prix Vermeille.

'She's a draw,' said owner Khalid Abdullah's racing manager Teddy Grimthorpe. 'She puts bums on seats and these are the people who pay for our great sport.'

Pre-race anxiety had increased when Enable became increasingly warm during the countdown to her latest mission. Even as she walked around the pre-parade ring moistness could be seen beneath the saddle, while by the time she reached the stalls the sweat had turned white.

Gosden later said that was of no concern, stating it was not unusual for her – although paddock judges could never remember her perspiring in the past – and pointing out sire Nathaniel had been a free sweater, which he absolutely was.

Should his daughter emulate him again in that regard we will be much less inclined to fret. Nor, following this all-the-way tour de force, will we start chomping on fingernails if on October 1 she has to make the running. Indeed, trying out the tactic here was one shrewd move.

With obvious Arc candidates far thinner on the ground than usual – Gosden also now has the second favourite in Cracksman, himself not guaranteed to join the party – this year's championship of Europe could have an unusually small field.

That, in turn, could produce a messy race, one that would not necessarily play to the strengths of a filly blessed with what Frankie Dettori called 'unbelievable stamina'.

Should the need arise, connections now know they can use that stamina to good effect by allowing Enable to roll along from the front.

Allowed to – Frankie called it 'floating' – and fired to the line a long way out, she came home with daylight to spare against high-class fillies.

This would have to be rated some way below her glorious Ascot defeat of the increasingly magnificent Ulysses, but it was also mission accomplished. Whether she could have done more had it been needed is immaterial. The day she may need to do more than she has ever done before is Arc day.

'If you don't care you don't get nervous, but these moments are there to be enjoyed,' said Grimthorpe. Whether Gosden enjoyed it quite so much is debatable, for he was quick to agree this was an afternoon when there was 'everything to lose'.

While speaking in the minutes after the King George he had also been clear in his belief that Enable is the best filly he has ever trained. The question of whether she is the best horse he has ever trained was indirectly put by Racing UK's Lydia Hislop when she asked him how he would compare his latest champion to Golden Horn, Gosden's Arc hero of two years ago.

With a slowness that implied a carefully considered answer, he said: 'She could look him in the eye – I don't know who would win.'

Nor does Gosden know who will win the Arc, but even though he described odds-on prices about Enable as 'silly' he would surely have to admit she will take some beating. That said, according to Grimthorpe, as a target looms ever closer Gosden's bullishness diminishes.

He may therefore have been seeking to start playing down expectations when, unexpectedly, he channeled the late Gorden 'Rene Artois' Kaye and delivered an anecdote on the subject of l'hippodrome de Chantilly.

Saying it only once, Gosden recalled: 'I said one day to Andre Fabre: "It's a beautiful track." He said [Gosden adopting a French accent]: "If I had my way I would blow it up. Quite often the best horse doesn't win".' On another highly enjoyable York afternoon, the best horse did win. Let's hope she also wins the Arc.

All roads led to the Arc after five successive victories, including four at Group 1 level, for Enable. She would now test herself against the best horses in Europe.

RACING POST RATINGS VIEW – **SAM WALKER**

Enable didn't need to run to her King George-winning best to easily land the Yorkshire Oaks.

She had 13lb in hand of her rivals on Racing Post Ratings going into the race and success was never in doubt.

She glided in by a cosy five lengths from stablemate Coronet (113), with Frankie Dettori reporting the winner was bored in front and had more in the tank.

A winning RPR of 121 ranks her up with the best recent winners of the Yorkshire Oaks, but we know she is capable of better.

Nothing has finished within four and a half lengths of Enable in her last four Group 1 wins and her peak performance from the King George (RPR 128) gained a further boost when Ulysses landed the Juddmonte International.

Enable will get a 1.5kg (3.3lb) sex allowance from the colts in the Prix de l'Arc de Triomphe, which means if she can run up to her best it would take a 132+ performance from a colt to beat her.

6356 **DARLEY YORKSHIRE OAKS (GROUP 1) (BRITISH CHAMPIONS SERIES) (F&M)** **1m 3f 188y**

3:35 (3:36) (Class 1) 3-Y-O+

£198,485 (£75,250; £37,660; £18,760; £9,415; £4,725) **Stalls** Centre

Form				Jockey	RPR
1111	**1**		**Enable**^{26} 5394 3-8-12 126 (John Gosden) *mde all: pushed along and qcknd 3f out: rdn clr wl over 1f out: kpt on strly: v readily* **1/4**^{1}	FrankieDettori 1	124+
3514	**2**	*5*	**Coronet**^{40} 4928 3-8-12 108 (John Gosden) *trckd ldng pair: hdwy over 2f out: rdn along wl over 1f out: kpt on fnl f: tk 2nd towards fin* **16/1**	OlivierPeslier 6	115
-446	**3**	*¾*	**Queen's Trust**^{21} 5571 4-9-7 118 (Sir Michael Stoute) *trckd wnr: effrt 3f out: rdn along 2f out: drvn over 1f out: kpt on same pce fnl f: lost 2nd towards fin* **12/1**^{3}	JimCrowley 2	114
11	**4**	*hd*	**Nezwaah**^{53} 4419 4-9-7 116 (Roger Varian) *hld up: hdwy wl over 2f out: rdn wl over 1f out: drvn and kpt on fnl f* **7/1**^{2}	AndreaAtzeni 4	113
3661	**5**	*9*	**Alluringly (USA)**^{8} 6080 3-8-12 105 (A P O'Brien, Ire) *.hld up in rr: effrt over 3f out: sn rdn along and n.d* **16/1**	RyanMoore 5	99
-123	**6**	*13*	**Abingdon (USA)**^{18} 5691 4-9-7 108 (Sir Michael Stoute) *trckd ldrs: pushed along 4f out: rdn over 3f out: outpcd and bhd fnl 2f* **33/1**	RichardKingscote 3	78

2m 35.79s (2.59) **Going Correction** +0.575s/f (Yiel)
WFA 3 from 4yo 9lb **6** Ran SP% **114.9**
Speed ratings (Par 117): **114,110,110,110,104 95**
CSF £6.66 TOTE £1.20: £1.10, £4.60; EX 5.20 Trifecta £27.00.
Owner K Abdullah **Bred** Juddmonte Farms Ltd **Trained** Newmarket, Suffolk

LONGINES
QATAR
PRIX DE L'ARC DE TRIOMPHE

SIX

PRIX DE L'ARC DE TRIOMPHE

Chantilly, October 1, 2017

Previous spread: Enable claims the first of two victories in the Prix de l'Arc de Triomphe at Chantilly in October 2017

3.05 *Qatar Prix de l'Arc de Triomphe (Group 1) (3yo+ No Geldings) (Turf)* **ITV**
Winner £2,441,880.34 **1m4f**

£4273504.27 guaranteed **For** 3yo+ no geldings **Weights** 3yo colts 8st 13lb; 3yo fillies 8st9lb; 4yo+ colts 9st 5lb; 4yo+ fillies/mares 9st2lb **Allowances** fillies & mares 1.5kg (3-4lb) **Entries** 121 **Penalty value 1st** £2,441,880.34 **2nd** £976,923.08 **3rd** £488,461.54 **4th** £244,017.09 **5th** £122,222.22

Form	No. (Draw)	Horse	Breeding	Trainer / Owner	Age Wgt	Jockey	RPR
3-14251	**1** (18)	**ZARAK** (FR) 91	*b c Dubawi-Zarkava*	**A de Royer-Dupre** H H Aga Khan	4 9-5	**Christophe Soumillon**	128
31-5U22	**2** (12)	**DOHA DREAM** (FR) 35	*b c Shamardal-Crystal Reef*	**A Fabre** Al Shaqab Racing	4 9-5	**Gregory Benoist**	122
613-722	**3** (11)	**ONE FOOT IN HEAVEN** (IRE) 15	*b h Fastnet Rock-Pride*	**A de Royer-Dupre** Fair Salinia Ltd	5 9-5	**James Doyle**	126
4-13121	**4** (1)	**ULYSSES** (IRE) 39	*ch c Galileo-Light Shift*	**Sir Michael Stoute (GB)** Flaxman Stables & Cheveley Park Stud	4 9-5	**Jim Crowley**	136
83-1112	**5** (3)	**CLOTH OF STARS** (IRE) 21	*b c Sea The Stars-Strawberry Fledge*	**A Fabre** Godolphin Snc	4 9-5	**Mickael Barzalona**	128
00-3125	**6** (16)	**SILVERWAVE** (FR) 21	*b h Silver Frost-Miss Bio*	**P Bary** Hspirit	5 9-5	**Pierre-Charles Boudot**	127
U5-6136	**7** (7)	**IDAHO** (IRE) 36	*b c Galileo-Hveger*	**A P O'Brien (IRE)** M Tabor & D Smith & Mrs J Magnier	4 9-5	**Seamie Heffernan**	131
1-15111	**8** (10)	**DSCHINGIS SECRET** (GER) 21	*b c Soldier Hollow-Divya*	**Markus Klug (GER)** Horst Pudwill	4 9-5	**Adrie de Vries**	130
111-134	**9** (13)	**SATONO DIAMOND** (JPN) 21	*b c Deep Impact-Malpensa*	**Yasutoshi Ikee (JPN)** Hajime Satomi	4 9-5	**Christophe-Patrice Lemaire**	133
2030-06	**10** (5)	**SATONO NOBLESSE** (JPN) 21	*b/br h Deep Impact-Cry With Joy*	**Yasutoshi Ikee (JPN)** Hajime Satomi	7 9-5	**Yuga Kawada**	123
47-2212	**11** (6)	**IQUITOS** (GER) 28	*b h Adlerflug-Irika*	**H-J Groschel (GER)** Stall Mulligan	5 9-5	**Andrasch Starke**	130
4-21211	**12** (9)	**ORDER OF ST GEORGE** (IRE) 21	*b h Galileo-Another Storm*	**A P O'Brien (IRE)** M Tabor/D Smith/Mrs Magnier/L J Williams	5 9-5	**Donnacha O'Brien**	134
154-219	**13** (17)	**SEVENTH HEAVEN** (IRE) 21	*b f Galileo-La Traviata*	**A P O'Brien (IRE)** D Smith & Mrs J Magnier & M Tabor	4 9-2	**Pat Smullen**	132
21-1115	**14** (4)	**BRAMETOT** (IRE) 47	*b c Rajsaman-Morning Light*	**J-C Rouget** Al Shaqab Racing & Gerard Augustin-Normand	3 8-13	**Cristian Demuro**	129
3-43611	**15** (15)	**CAPRI** (IRE) 15	*gr c Galileo-Dialafara*	**A P O'Brien (IRE)** D Smith & Mrs J Magnier & M Tabor	3 8-13	**Wayne Lordan**	129
1202	**16** (14)	**PLUMATIC** 15	*b c Dubawi-Plumania*	**A Fabre** Wertheimer & Frere	3 8-13	**Maxime Guyon**	125
-311111	**17** (2)	**ENABLE** 38	*b f Nathaniel-Concentric*	**John Gosden (GB)** K Abdullah	3 8-9	**Frankie Dettori**	140
-211112	**18** (8)	**WINTER** (IRE) 22	*gr f Galileo-Laddies Poker Two*	**A P O'Brien (IRE)** Mrs John Magnier & Michael Tabor & Derrick Smith	3 8-9	**Ryan Moore**	131

2016 (16 ran) **Found** (12) A P O'Brien 4 9-2 6/1 Ryan Moore RPR124

BETTING FORECAST: Evens Enable, 7 Ulysses, 8 Winter, 10 Order Of St George, 12 Dschingis Secret, 14 Brametot, 16 Capri, 20 Zarak, 25 Idaho, Satono Diamond, 33 Cloth Of Stars, 40 Seventh Heaven, 66 Iquitos, One Foot In Heaven, Plumatic, Silverwave, 100 Doha Dream, 200 Satono Noblesse.

ENABLE CAME OUT of York in good shape and John Gosden said the plan was to go straight to the Prix de l'Arc de Triomphe. Europe's most prestigious race was being run at Chantilly for a second time in 2017 while Longchamp was being redeveloped.

The only question that remained unanswered for Gosden was whether Enable would be joined by stablemate Cracksman. Anthony Oppenheimer's son of Frankel, who had been placed in the Derby and Irish Derby as well as winning the Great Voltigeur and Prix Niel, was under serious consideration for the Arc.

However, connections decided to aim Cracksman at the Champion Stakes at Ascot and that left the way open for Enable to head to Chantilly as a firm favourite. First, Alastair Down spoke to Gosden about her career:

An illuminating hour and a half with John Gosden contained something of a revelation. For all the plaudits the trainer has received for handling the genuinely exceptional Enable, the truth emerges that he doesn't train her at all – she trains him.

Twice this season Gosden has departed from his script for Enable because she rewrote it for him. It was as if she said: 'Now Gosden, you and I need to sit down and have a word about where I'm going next.' Prince Khalid Abdullah should ask for a rebate on the training fees.

'It was never the original plan to run her in the King George, not least because it came just two weeks after the Irish Oaks,' says Gosden.

'But I did something a little different when sending her to Ireland. As a rule ours go over by road, but it's a long way to Holyhead and then there's the ferry. It adds up to a taxing 16-hour haul.

'Unusually we flew her to Ireland, and taking the plane made the whole performance less arduous and in no time after the race she was bouncing again.

'So we went to the King George and it was a tough race as they geared it up plenty early on and then going into the bend they really went – and all in that ground too.'

Robert Havlin and Enable on the Newmarket gallops in September 2017

Running on loose ground for the first time, Enable trounced the older horses and beat Ulysses – an Eclipse behind him and the Juddmonte International still ahead – by four and a half lengths. A star had been born at Epsom, twinkled further on the Curragh and shot up into the firmament at Ascot.

'It was at least half my intention to go straight to the Arc but in early August she dropped Mr Dettori one morning and was so well in herself that we decided to go to York.'

What he means is that Enable decided she fancied the job. 'There wasn't much early pace at York so Frankie just let her do her own thing and bowl along from the front. He said she got bored in front but that didn't stop her winning five lengths.'

Part of Enable's weaponry is the sheer stamp of her. She is not a physical freak but she is an exceptional example of the racehorse nonetheless, and has been from day one. She didn't run as a two-year-old until late November, winning on Newcastle's all-weather

– a course Gosden likes because that straight mile produces evenly run races.

'When she first came to us you saw straight away that she had this incredible body,' he says.

'She had real depth of girth – space for an engine room or heart room. And when they're like that you have the chance they have a seriously powerful cardio-vascular system. Even with a small horse you're looking for that depth to them.

'The reason she was late making her debut was that she did a lot of growing and that's when you have to back off them.

'Horses keep growing to the age of five – they don't even have all the teeth until they're four. Sea The Stars grew plenty after he went to stud and so did Enable's sire Nathaniel. It's not surprising because at three horses are the equivalent of a 16- or 17-year-old and not yet fully mature.'

As well as having more depth to her than the Mariana Trench, Enable also has notably large lugs. If they ever write an equine version of the dreadful Noddy books she'd be a shoo-in for Big Ears.

Enable and Robert Havlin canter up Warren Hill two days before her first victory in the Prix de l'Arc de Triomphe

Robert Havlin and Enable with John Gosden on the Newmarket gallops

Gosden's fears the Arc revolve around potential traffic problems and the course itself. He is worried more about the place than the race.

'I would be more confident if the race was at Longchamp, where you can steady it down the hill into the false straight.

'To Chantilly's credit they've done a brilliant job to keep the course in such good condition given all the extra racing there has been there, but it's a narrow track and, exaggerating a little, it has this banked hairpin bend. If you go too fast round there you'll end up in the lake in front of the chateau. As Andre Fabre is fond of saying, "Quite often the best horse doesn't win there".

'Happily, we're not drawn in the car park, but we'll need luck in running. I am concerned about the run of the race and I'm very clear in my mind that she's had quite a lot of racing this season. But her work at home is bridle work and amazingly she's weighing in now as big as ever.

'The scales tell you plenty – as you and I know! What's more, she has taken all her races very well because she has a very good constitution – it's that depth again.

'She's a charming filly, a playful one. If she worked here she would always walk into the yard humming a tune. She enjoys life, enjoys her exercise and she likes to please.

'And where and when she runs is more her idea than mine sometimes.'

Enable is a product of Khalid Abdullah's Juddmonte operation, which, pound for pound, has to be the most successful bloodstock empire of the modern era. Gosden says: 'I first met Prince Khalid at Jeremy Tree's well over 30 years ago. He really knows his families and let's the trainer train them.

'He has developed his own families and bloodlines and it has all been achieved since 1980 – not even 40 years. He has the most fantastic farms that have been instrumental in his success and I can't emphasise enough how exceptional the people are who work on the farms.

'In those very early stages with horses it's all about nurturing and Juddmonte's staff are incredible stockmen, so you know where you are when the yearlings come to you.

'And of course you get to know your families, which stops you repeating mistakes with them you may have made in the past. I don't want to get in trouble for saying so but it's a little bit like insider trading. But respectable!'

We break off to watch a colt by Frankel – the towering colossus of Juddmonte's short history – go through the ring at the Goffs Orby sale.

Gosden, 66, has recently taken on the considerable added responsibility of approving Godolphin's sales purchases. Nothing gets bought without his seal of approval.

With Gosden on the phone to his team ringside, they go to €1.5 million but are underbidder to Coolmore's clinching bid of €1.6m.

He has some interesting asides on Frankel. 'I have no doubt Frankel kept Henry alive and he handled him brilliantly because the horse could be very aggressive.

'If you said to him, "Don't gallop through that brick wall," he would gallop straight through it. His progeny outstay their pedigree but – how shall I put this? – some Frankels can be a touch over-exuberant.'

Frankel stands at Banstead Manor Stud just outside Newmarket and that in itself is a reflection of the swift evolution of racing in recent decades.

Gosden, forever a man for the bigger picture, says: 'There have been huge changes for Newmarket since 1980. Prior to that if we had Classic winners here they would go straight off to Kentucky at the age of three. That left the world's best grass pedigrees in America.

'Then suddenly, with massive investment from the Middle East and the likes of Cheveley Park Stud, the good stallions stayed in Britain and Ireland and all the best mares went to them.

'It upgraded quality no end, and it helped to invigorate Newmarket. Back in the 1970s we had the three-day week and endless power cuts. Half the yards were empty and it became a bit of a ghost town. Now there are horses in training everywhere and just down the road we have Cambridge, which is the fastest-growing city in the UK.

'But the wider landscape is changing too, not least in the betting industry, and I would like to see further harmony between bookmaking and racing.

'Betting, like everything else, is going online. Betting shops will be like speakeasys and there will come a time when high streets will have shops shut like we suddenly had with empty branches of Dewhursts.

'A few years ago one of the big bookmaking bosses told me that if he could have two more machines in every shop then racing could have what it wanted on the money front.

'It's probably amoral that betting shops are now dependent on people who can't leave a machine alone.'

From discussing the wider world, the trainer refocuses on the immediate job in hand, Enable's Arc bid with Frankie Dettori doing the steering and project managing the vital task of keeping his filly out of trouble in a race that can often be rough.

Though I have never heard Gosden mention it, he was the man who moulded and tamed Dettori in his early days. What is more, he has always been the man who carried out the running repairs and restoration when the mercurial sardine was out of sorts or professionally on his uppers.

Gosden says: 'Pound for pound, Frankie is the greatest I've ever seen when he's in the zone. If he's content in his mind he can ride at another level.

'He's here every day and we're like an extension of his family. It's a serious business but he loves all the banter and he's got a big heart.

'What's more, he's very good in the morning – and I've known great jockeys who were absolutely hopeless in the mornings. What they said was always misleading for the simple reason that they couldn't read a gallop. They were good on course but useless at home.

'As a trainer you're always trying to conserve a horse's energy, fitness and wellbeing for the race but plenty of jockeys want to find out that little bit.

'Lester Piggott was famous for that, which is why Vincent O'Brien was never mad about him riding work at Ballydoyle. It's part of many a jockey's nature. It's just like you or I hiring a rental car with a big engine – you can't resist giving it a bit of welly. Frankie spares us all that.'

Gosden is almost incredulous when discussing the Juddmonte families and describes their inception, growth and pre-eminence as 'one of the greatest achievements of our time'.

Yet as a wizard when it comes to a Hunt Cup or a Cambridgeshire, he could not resist once saying to Prince Khalid: 'I'm afraid yours are bad handicapping colours, sir, nobody is going to miss those white sleeves.'

But this afternoon we expect to see those white sleeves rampant rather than being discreet.

Gosden smiles. 'I remember Frankie saying, after the Irish Oaks, "To sit on something like this is exhilarating. And for her to come so soon after Golden Horn, well, I can't believe our luck".'

Here's to that luck holding on this day of days.

We were the lucky ones as Enable delivered in style. Lee Mottershead reported from Chantilly:

Frankie Dettori is the most famous jockey in the world and now boasts more wins in the world's most prestigious Flat race than any man in history, yet this was a day when even he was upstaged by his leading lady as the indisputably magnificent Enable annihilated all opposition in the Prix de l'Arc de Triomphe.

Less than a year after making her debut in a winter all-weather maiden at Newcastle, the towering four-legged figure of European Flat racing dazzled on the greatest possible stage, unleashing an irresistible surge of acceleration that left her gloriously out on her own.

Since finishing third to a stablemate at Newbury in April, the latest superstar in Khalid Abdullah's breeding empire had won the Oaks, Irish Oaks, King George VI and Queen Elizabeth Stakes and Yorkshire Oaks by a combined total of 20 lengths.

Enable and Frankie Dettori come home two and a half lengths clear of Cloth Of Stars (blue silks) in the Arc

Indeed, such has been her superiority over all those she has faced, racegoers at Chantilly sent her off odds-on favourite for what should have been a fierce test but instead turned into the latest tour de force.

When passing the post two and a half lengths ahead of Cloth Of Stars, with old rival Ulysses in third, Enable became the first British-trained filly to land the Qatar-sponsored Arc and, 29 years on from his debut Arc appearance, Dettori secured a record-breaking fifth success in a showpiece that for its 96th running carried a first prize of nearly £2.5 million.

A sizeable chunk of the cash will be paid to the 46-year-old rider and trainer John Gosden, who just two years ago had combined with Golden Horn to win the final Arc staged at Longchamp in its old form.

Now, in 12 months' time, there must be a big chance Enable will seek to emulate another fabulous female, Treve, by completing back-to-back triumphs as this sporting institution is held at the new Longchamp for the first time.

'She is magnificent,' said Gosden.

His assessment could not be challenged, while he could not deny the final countdown had been deeply stressful.

'It's been hellish,' he said. 'You watch the filly every moment and are in danger of wearing down a path from your back door to her box. It's the expectation, so when she wins like that it's a relief and you can really enjoy it.

'She can cruise and then put in a massive turn of foot. Her acceleration kills off a field. She's done it before and done it today.

'She has a great mind on her as well. She enjoys training and still looks good in her summer coat, even though the autumn leaves are coming off.

'She is a majestic queen of a filly, and like Treve she has big ears. We like big ears.'

Dettori also likes Enable's ears and indeed every part of what he described as the best filly he has ridden.

On this occasion he rode her prominently, just in behind front-running Ballydoyle pair Idaho and Order Of St George. So well was she travelling at the top of the home straight that he could contain her no longer.

With two furlongs to run he allowed her to do what she was plainly desperate to do. She did it in style, settling the Arc in exhilarating fashion.

John Gosden congratulates Enable and Frankie Dettori after their Arc victory

'I was quite emotional and able to enjoy it because it happened so easily,' said Dettori, whose first Arc triumph had come in 1995 on Lammtarra.

'C'est magnifique. She's a tremendous filly. Usually in an Arc something happens but it was so smooth and so effortless. I was quite shocked. Then you ask yourself, 'I'm not actually dreaming? This is true, isn't it?'

It was true, which delighted Dettori, as did the fact he had moved to the top of the Arc's alltime winning jockey list.

'Yes!' he exclaimed in the post-race press conference. 'I'm the first to get to five and it's a great achievement. I've had 29 goes at it, so five is not that great a strike-rate!

'Every one of them is special but when you ride an odds-on favourite in the Arc, well, even I was nervous – but if you're not nervous you're not human.'

The human who will determine whether Enable races next year – Gosden made clear he would not wish to run her again this season – is Abdullah, whose racing manager Teddy Grimthorpe said: 'This is a question we've been asked quite a lot. Really we'd just like to see the filly back home and then we can ask Prince Khalid what he'd like to do next year.'

To see the faces of Dettori and Gosden as they spoke, it was obvious their dearest wish is that Enable is allowed to compete at four.

At three she has been a joy to watch, never more so than on the afternoon when she made Chantilly's final Arc one to live long in the memory.

Dettori described how he won a record-breaking fifth Arc:

Before the race I was toying with the idea of making the running, but I was aware Idaho, Capri and Order Of St George are good stayers.

There's a little tower by the 2,000-metre mark and that was my first marker. I said to John Gosden: "I have 400 metres to really find out what's going to happen."

I went to make the running but I saw Idaho was running free so let him slot in. Then I could see Order Of St George breathing down my quarters, so I checked behind him and there was plenty of room. I managed to drag her back and get behind Order Of St George.

At that moment I was exactly where I wanted her to be, with free air on my left. It got to the point where I was running away around the bend. I was striking Order Of St George's heels; I was going that well and I could see distress signals from the one in front.

I thought at York I perhaps went a little too soon so I counted to ten. I couldn't wait to get to the 400-metre mark and when I got there I

Frankie Dettori acknowledges the crowd after winning the Arc on Enable

asked her to go and she flew. She's got a burst of three or four lengths and then sustains it.

When we plateaued at that speed I was just counting the furlong discs – it was so smooth and so effortless.

Enable deserves all the credit. She is the best filly I've ever ridden and John is a genius. He kept her at absolutely top shape all year.

I'm the first jockey to get to five Arc wins and I'm very proud of today – it hasn't sunk in yet. I'm looking forward to a nice glass of something tonight.

Enable lit up Chantilly with a win worthy of any stage according to Tom Kerr:

This was likely to have been the last Prix de l'Arc de Triomphe ever staged at Chantilly but Enable ensured the race's brief sojourn at the spiritual home of French racing will forever be remembered as the scene of a breathtaking victory by a filly who with one thunderous burst of acceleration wrote her name into racing's foremost ranks.

Chantilly's spell as the home of the Arc was already notable on a number of levels. It had introduced the loyal legion of British and Irish racegoers who treat Arc weekend as an annual pilgrimage to a jewel in the crown of European racing, a boutique track that emerges from amid thick forest like some sacred grove, France's temple to the horse.

And last year, in the first Arc to be held at Chantilly, Aidan O'Brien delivered one of those epic racing feats that defy belief but which

Enable wins the Arc at Chantilly under Frankie Dettori

seemingly flow effortlessly from his hands, as his great female warrior Found led home a 1-2-3 in the race, a display of pan-European dominance that would have done Charlemagne proud.

O'Brien sent the entirety of the 1st Ballydoyle Hussars to Chantilly this year, five of his finest lining up in an 18-runner Arc. He has had a season of wonders, winning eight of the ten British and Irish Classics among a host of other prizes, but there has been one exceptional filly who denied him a clean sweep of Classics and it was none other than her who wowed Chantilly with a performance for the ages.

Enable came to Chantilly with a British and Irish Oaks, a King George and a Yorkshire Oaks already under her belt; it has been a marauding, devastating season in which Enable has thrashed fillies, colts and older horses alike, sweeping home each time with rivals toiling far behind her.

Combining a punishing cruising speed with whip-fast acceleration, she came to Chantilly as the standout horse of 2017 and was sent off the first odds-on favourite since Sea The Stars in 2009.

Still, nothing is ever supposed to be straightforward in the Arc. This was Enable's greatest test and it fell at the end of a long, hard season. She faced the cream from within Europe's middle-distance division and a smattering of wildcards from without. And she was drawn in gate two, just off the rail, a precarious position from which her rider Frankie Dettori might find himself penned in.

It was this last fear that almost came to pass, with Enable leaping lively out of the gate and into a prominent position but soon finding herself in danger of being pinned within a Ballydoyle pincer, with Idaho in front and Order Of St George on her flank. Dettori was having none of it; he switched back, swung outside and was breathing clear air once more. How sweet it must have been.

John Gosden was fairly rapturous in his praise of Dettori's manoeuvre immediately after the race but later, when the two sat down together to give a press conference, he set to teasing him, declaring: 'I'm very pleased for a young and up-and-coming jockey like him to use his head as he did.'

Dettori, now 46, has said before that he intends to ride to 50 at least and this observer reckons if horses like this keep coming along he'll still be doing it in his dotage. This was a reminder of how sorely the sport will feel his retirement when that day eventually comes.

Not only is he a master of his craft but a showman par excellence, who whipped the crowd – French, British, Irish, German

A delighted Frankie Dettori jumps from Enable in the Chantilly winner's enclosure

and Japanese alike – into a distinctly un-Parisian frenzy as he and Enable made their triumphant way back to the winner's enclosure.

Dettori is a superstar but the heroine of this race was Enable. She has been wowing the sport since slamming her Oaks rivals in the midst of a thunderstorm in June and has only gone from strength to strength since.

The weather was more drizzle than driving rain but Enable delivered her own lightning bolt a furlong and a half out, dazzling Chantilly with a burst of acceleration that carried her instantly clear of her rivals and into an unassailable lead.

'She's brilliant, she travels so well, she's a very exciting and majestic filly,' said Gosden, who would not be drawn on whether Enable will remain in training as a four-year-old but who did talk, hypothetically but with a hint of hope, about the prospect of Enable returning to the new Longchamp next year to defend her crown.

Many will be glad to return to Longchamp, not least the French. They gave Chantilly a wide berth last year and, although it appeared the crowd was about half made up of locals, they were given nothing to cheer about: British and Irish horses carried off all six Group 1 races, from Wild Illusion's win in the Marcel Boussac through to

Aclaim's victory in the concluding Foret. French pride has been dealt a few knocks in the heat of battle over the years and this was up there with Waterloo.

Yet Chantilly has been an enchanting temporary home for Europe's greatest race. It may not have Longchamp's size or central location, but it has beauty, history and charm in abundance.

Most crucially, it has played host to two Arcs worthy of any stage: one a team performance of almost inconceivable dominance, the other an individual triumph of a filly who has lit up Flat racing, no matter how dreary the skies she raced beneath.

Adieu Chantilly, we shan't forget you.

Enable had achieved something no other British-trained filly had done as James Burn reported:

In winning yesterday's Qatar Prix de l'Arc de Triomphe, Enable went where no other British-trained filly or mare had gone before by becoming the first to capture Europe's richest race.

Her trainer John Gosden would have been well aware of the task at hand having saddled Taghrooda (third in 2014), Great Heavens (sixth in 2012) and Dar Re Mi (fifth in 2009) in recent Arcs, while Ed Dunlop was responsible for Snow Fairy and Ouija Board filling third in 2011 and 2004.

Before Enable, Legera had come closest to ending Britain's female Arc curse in 1998. Trained by Dunlop's father John, she pushed Sagamix to a neck and was also fourth the following year to the mighty Montjeu.

Another near miss for British-trained females came in 1992 when the Clive Brittain-trained User Friendly, who like Enable had won the Oaks, Irish Oaks and Yorkshire Oaks as well as the St Leger, was beaten a neck by Subotica – two years earlier the high-class and well-fancied Salsabil ran no race at Longchamp, finishing tenth of 21 runners.

Sun Princess, trained by Dick Hern and ridden by Willie Carson, also finished second in the Arc, going down to a Walter Swinburn-inspired All Along in the 1983 edition, while 4-1 second favourite Park Top was a fast-finishing runner-up to Levmoss in 1969.

Dettori later spoke about Enable's success as Stuart Riley reported:

Ryan Moore was on the receiving end of Frankie Dettori's post-Arc lip service last year but this time Enable was sole subject of his affections as his historic Chantilly-winning partner proved the perfect morning-after cure.

Winning the Prix de l'Arc de Triomphe for a record-breaking fifth time was the spark for celebrations that left Dettori feeling a shade delicate.

But a visit to see Enable did the trick as he laid a smacker on 'the best filly I've ever ridden' when greeting the daughter of Nathaniel on her return to John Gosden's Clarehaven Stables in Newmarket with a packet of Polos and a big hug.

The world's most famous jockey is often on the receiving end of selfie requests but even celebrities have their idols and Enable is such a superstar in Dettori's eyes that even he was compelled to grab a few snaps for posterity.

'I've felt better, but it's all self-inflicted!' said Dettori after waking up the most decorated rider in the history of the Arc following the pair's sensational triumph at Chantilly.

'I've just been to see Enable now, I gave her a few Polos and a big kiss on the mouth,' he said. 'She had a nice roll in her box with her Arc de Triomphe-winning rug on. I even got some pictures.'

Frankie Dettori can't stop smiling after landing the Arc on Enable

Dettori, who congratulated Moore with a kiss after his weighing-room colleague won the Arc on Found in 2016, was still revelling in a success so fine that it brought Gosden close to tears.

He said about the five-time Group 1 winner: 'She's without a doubt the best filly I've ever ridden. It's very hard to compare years, and colts with fillies, but she's definitely as good as I've ridden.

'It'd be very unfair to say best, or better, because I've ridden some great horses, but she's up there with the best of them.'

The esteem in which Dettori holds the two-and-a-half-length winner means he is among those clamouring to see her race on again next season aged four, a hope shared by Gosden.

He said: 'She's been amazing all year and what a ride she is, she's a jockey's dream. Of course I'd love her to come back, we can try to do what Treve did and win the Arc again.'

Dettori and Gosden may take encouragement from the fact owner Khalid Abdullah sportingly campaigned his last superstar mare Midday until she was five. He also forsook a year of stud fees to give Frankel one more season to establish his position as the greatest of all time.

But while his racing manager Teddy Grimthorpe would not commit to anything, he also ruled nothing out.

'She was fine this morning and yesterday was very special – as a victory it was hugely important to us,' he said. 'It was Frankie's fifth Arc, Prince Khalid's fifth Arc and Enable's fifth Group 1. It was certainly a tremendous performance.

'We'll see how she is and I'll talk to Prince Khalid in good time – but there's no hurry for that decision.'

All parties have agreed that she will not run again this season. Bookmakers make her a 7-2 shot to emulate Treve and win next year's Arc, which will be run back at its traditional home, Longchamp, after a two-year absence.

Enable's Arc victory had Alastair Down in raptures:

After the Arc came the Prix de l'Opera, but there was no need for the fat lady even to clear her throat – she was redundant. The lady with the big ears had already sung and hit all the high notes with consummate ease.

Being a jumps man to the inner core, it is rare for a Flat race to get the emotions fizzing – winter for the heart, summer for the head – but this triumph leapt across that divide, and joyously so.

Frankie Dettori celebrates after crossing the line on Enable in the Arc

Enable's triumph under a master steer from Frankie Dettori, still irrepressible at the age of 46, tapped straight into the soul. Frankie had the race won in the first 200 yards. His draw in stall two meant that if he got trapped on the rail the next mile and a half could have been all about him trying desperately to push up the coffin lid as the rest of the field, including five Ballydoyle bruisers, hammered nails into it.

Hell bent on not being mugged, Dettori smoothly arrowed Enable out to position A-plus. From that moment Chantilly changed from being a racecourse to a path to glory.

Enable can quicken like a pulse and when she kicked just before the two-furlong pole it was indeed all over bar the shouting – and my

God, there was plenty of that. Hard though it was to take your eyes off the filly, a stolen glance behind showed every jockey not called Dettori was slapping and scrubbing away like those poor so-and-sos who have to do their washing on a rock down by the riverside.

The absurdly talented and mercurial Dettori, nurtured by John Gosden every bit as much as Enable, cannot be matched at moments like these. He milked the victory more than a Somerset dairy farmer and I defy anyone to say they did not find his storm force ten celebrations anything other than infectious and engaging. Dettori is no stranger to dark places but like some unbeatable escapologist, he always extricates himself from his troubles.

No other jockey has ever had Frankie's power to engage the racing public. When he throws open his arms it is to embrace us all and what he is saying is: 'This is my world – welcome to it.' He gives us a flavour, ahead of someone armed with a mic asking him, of what it truly feels like. We owe him thanks for that.

Beaming and elated, with a smile wider than the Seine, he jumped – literally – through the rituals of his happy post-race pantomime. But there came a moment on the presentation podium, as the national anthem was played, that his face turned stoneface serious. You could almost hear him thinking.

Maybe it was plain emotion, perhaps some reflection on the roads travelled. To see it told you that not a second of the afternoon was going unmarked and also prompted you to recall that there are such things as the tears of a clown.

In his brief press conference after the tumult and the shouting had died Dettori said: 'Even I was nervous, if you're not nervous you're not living. Usually something happens to you in an Arc but it was smooth and effortless.'

When congratulated on his record fifth win he darted back: 'Well, I have had 29 attempts!' I reckon a 17 per cent strike-rate in the Arc is more than a triomphe, and there must also be case for this being Gosden's finest hour. To keep a filly on the go from April to October without a break is not the stuff of simplicity.

Yes she has a Churchillian constitution – the great man drank 42,000 bottles of Pol Roger but still lived to 90 – but it is also a question of keeping Enable's mind sweet as a nut. Gosden calls her a charming filly, but that is because she has been charmed.

What is staggering about Enable is the margin of her victories. Her previous four Group 1 triumphs had a cumulative winning margin of

20 lengths. In our sport we measure superiority in distances and she has been operating on another plateau.

Okay, Sunday was a trifling two and a half, but it was the Arc and I thought Frankie was rehearsing his victory speech from a furlong out. She could have won by more.

Enable has been Gosden's masterpiece. She went to Chantilly weighing more than she had all season – something that could be said of many who watched. For me, she is up there with the likes of Dahlia, Allez France, Zarkava and Treve from my time. And possibly ahead of at least two of those immortals.

Gosden is clearly going to try to persuade Prince Khalid – whose love of French racing dates back to his student days – to keep Enable in training at four.

That is something devoutly to be hoped and I suspect he will not have to push hard at the door – it is probably already ajar. You can't guarantee that she will be as dazzlingly brilliant next season but my goodness, it would be wonderful to have a peek.

She has become a destination horse – one who must be visited and seen. If you have not done so then make sure of putting that right if we are blessed with another year of this ace who puts all her rivals in a hole.

Gosden reflected on Enable's fantastic year and discussed the possibility of her remaining in training as a four-year-old as David Baxter reported:

A decision on whether Prix de l'Arc de Triomphe heroine Enable will return to training at four has yet to be made, but she would be welcomed back with open arms by trainer John Gosden, who hailed the filly's spectacular achievement.

Gosden was at the Tattersalls yearling sales trying to find stars of the future, but he already has a superstar at home in Enable, who made it five Group 1 wins in a row with a sublime performance at Chantilly.

Having been visited on Monday by big-race partner Frankie Dettori, Enable has settled back in to life at Clarehaven Stables in Newmarket, and Gosden said: 'She's in great form. She got back in very good order and had a trot and pick of grass this morning. She's got a little cut on a hind leg from the race but is fine.'

Boasting a CV bulging with big-race wins, the daughter of Nathaniel will be a hot commodity when she does make it to the

Frankie Dettori salutes the crowd at Chantilly after Enable's Arc success

breeding sheds, but when exactly that will happen is still open to discussion.

'She's done everything we could have dreamed of,' Gosden added. 'We'll see how she is over the next ten days and talk to Prince Khalid, who will make a decision. She's only really had ten months of racing and it would be wonderful if she could run next season as she would be bit of a crowd-puller.'

Gosden watched the race in splendid isolation from what was already his favourite grandstand at Chantilly and, reflecting on the afternoon, he said: 'It was very moving. There was an awful lot of pressure and a lot was expected.'

That pressure melted away as Dettori helped deliver the seventh victory of Enable's eight-race career and the trainer now has the pleasant problem of whether she, like 2015 Arc winner Golden Horn, will have a statue on the lawn at the yard to commemorate her achievement.

He added: 'She's a very kind filly with a lovely, sweet nature, but when she gets her tack on she's very assertive. She was expressing herself and it was great for her and for Prince Khalid.'

Dettori's part in the Enable story could not be underplayed as Steve Dennis wrote in the days following the Arc:

You would not think, to look at him at Chantilly on Sunday afternoon, that he was all but finished not long ago. Like the great showman he is, Frankie Dettori is revelling – as do we – in encore after encore.

Here he is at 46, rising 47, partnering the filly he describes as the best he's ever ridden (although let's hope Ouija Board isn't listening), and doing so in what might be quietly termed the autumn of his magnificent career.

If Enable truly is his best filly then she is all the more remarkable for arriving at this stage of his racing life. Good horses come along every now and then but there can only be one 'best'.

Two years ago Dettori called Golden Horn 'probably the best I've ridden' (let's hope Dubai Millennium and Daylami aren't listening) but it's not the exuberant post-race hyperbole that needs attention but the fact that these twin peaks on his personal landscape have appeared now.

Of course, the record books are replete with elderly jockeys riding champions to great glory.

George Duffield was 50 when he won the Eclipse on Giant's Causeway, the same age as Mick Kinane when he enjoyed the annus mirabilis of Sea The Stars, a year younger than Mike Smith aboard Arrogate, and all years younger than the incomparable Lester Piggott, 56 in the year of Rodrigo De Triano. And as medical provision continues to improve and we all supposedly face the desperately unpleasant scenario of living past 100 it may become a more common occurrence.

But what captivates is the scale of the feast following the scale of the famine. Lest we forget, four years ago Dettori was in danger of fading away before our very eyes. In the catty, bitchy, all-too-human attachment to the fickleness of fashion, the Italian was dungarees, he was legwarmers. When he slipped back in through the out door after a six-month suspension for failing a drug test, he reckoned that he was 'starting from scratch again'. And it was a slow start.

Sixteen winners in Britain in 2013, 37 winners in Britain in 2014. Those who thought they knew nodded sagely to each other and muttered about having seen the best of old Frankie. Wonder what he'll do now? Another pizza restaurant? Bit of media work? Shame, really, he was such a good jockey once.

Racing steeled itself to live without its ringmaster. The only Flat jockey anyone outside the bubble had ever heard of was drifting out of earshot.

And then along came Golden Horn, and Galileo Gold, and Lady Aurelia, and now Enable. Circumstance had plenty to do with it, naturally, but that's life.

If Anthony Oppenheimer had sold Golden Horn at auction instead of taking him home again when the price wasn't right, the colt probably wouldn't have found his way to John Gosden, and some other jockey would have won the Derby, Eclipse and Arc.

If Gosden hadn't resuscitated his old pals' act with Dettori, if Sheikh Joaan Al Thani hadn't become his new friend, what might have been? If, a small word so enormous that it changes all of our lives, was about to change Dettori's. And we all love redemption stories because they foster the hope it might happen to us too. Golden Horn and Enable were Dettori's redemption. Someone up there must like him.

It is worth waiting for, the best filly you've ever ridden. Some jockeys find their best filly at 22, like Billy Newnes and Time Charter. Some get theirs a little later; Steve Cauthen at 25, with Oh So Sharp, or 32-year-old Yves Saint-Martin and Allez France. Some later still, Willie Carson at 40, and Sun Princess. Dettori had to wait until well into his 46th year, beyond the milestone of 3,000 winners, beyond the realms of probability, and the wonder of it was that she came at all.

Ouija Board would have been enough, or Balanchine, enough to gild the conversation of old age when the hacks came to drag him off down memory lane. How remarkable it is that the best is saved until almost last, a living demonstration of the virtues of patience and perseverance, of the rare vanquishing of experience by hope.

At his lowest ebb, Dettori would not have dreamed of an Enable. Yet there he was, guiding her unerringly to one of the most straightforward Arc wins on record, all point and press and practice the chatter for the press conference. He says he might go on to 50, or longer. The showman must go on. There is still time to find a better one than even this filly.

Gosden's decision not to run Cracksman in the Arc paid off when he demolished his rivals in the Champion Stakes. It was a standout year for Enable with five victories at the top level and she was named Cartier Horse of the Year. The news that she would stay in training in 2018 was something for every racing fan to look forward to.

RACING POST RATINGS VIEW – SAM WALKER

Enable ranks among the best Arc winners of recent years after scoring with total authority. A Racing Post Rating of 129 puts the three-year-old level with the unbeaten 2008 winner Zarkava and 2lb behind the mighty Treve, who beat Orfevre by five lengths to land her first Arc in 2013.

A figure of 129 also moves Enable up among the leading seven fillies and mares worldwide since 2000.

Khalid Abdullah's filly was always close to the pace at Chantilly, travelled strongly into the lead with two furlongs to go and by the furlong pole she was three lengths clear.

A combination of idling and easing inside the final furlong meant the winning margin of two and a half lengths over Cloth Of Stars (126) slightly underplays her superiority.

The form looks as solid as ever for Europe's premier race, as the next six horses behind Enable were all Group 1 winners.

7668a **QATAR PRIX DE L'ARC DE TRIOMPHE (GROUP 1) (3YO+ NO GELDINGS) (TURF)** **1m 4f**
3:05 3-Y-O+ **£2,441,880** (£976,923; £488,461; £244,017; £122,222)

			RPR
1		**Enable**38 6356 3-8-9 0 .... FrankieDettori 2 (John Gosden) *a handy: angled out to chse ldng pair ins fnl 2 1/2f: qcknd to ld under 2f out: rdn clr 1 1/2f out: styd on strly* **10/11**1	129+
2	*2 ½*	**Cloth Of Stars (IRE)**21 6983 4-9-5 0 .... MickaelBarzalona 3 (A Fabre, France) *settled in midfield: gd hdwy over 1 1/2f out: drvn and styd on to go 2nd 110yds fr home: no ch w wnr* **20/1**	126
3	*1 ¼*	**Ulysses (IRE)**39 6328 4-9-5 0 .... JimCrowley 1 (Sir Michael Stoute) *racd a little freely early: a.p: trckd eventual wnr through 2f out: rdn to go 2nd appr fnl f but unable to keep tabs on wnr: kpt on fnl f: lost 2nd 110yds fr home: no ex* **9/1**3	124
4	*1 ½*	**Order Of St George (IRE)**21 6976 5-9-5 0 .... DonnachaO'Brien 9 (A P O'Brien, Ire) *a cl up: 2nd and scrubbed along 2 1/2f out: chsd ldrs fr 2f out: styd on wout having pce to chal* **8/1**2	122
5	*1 ¼*	**Brametot (IRE)**47 6053 3-8-13 0 .... CristianDemuro 4 (J-C Rouget, France) *cl up on inner: 4th and drvn 2 1/2f out: no imp wl over 1 1/2f out: kpt on u.p fnl f* **20/1**	121
6	*½*	**Dschingis Secret (GER)**21 6983 4-9-5 0 .... AdriedeVries 10 (Markus Klug, Germany) *w.w in midfield on outer: 5th and travelling wl enough 3f out: scrubbed along in pursuit of ldrs 2f out: sn rdn and no imp: kpt on same pce fnl f* **14/1**	119
7	*hd*	**Iquitos (GER)**28 6727 5-9-5 0 .... AndraschStarke 6 (H-J Groschel, Germany) *towards rr: hdwy 2f out: styd on u.p fnl 1 1/2f: nvr nrr* **100/1**	118+
8	*nse*	**Idaho (IRE)**36 6461 4-9-5 0 .... SeamieHeffernan 7 (A P O'Brien, Ire) *led: drvn ins fnl 2 1/2f: hdd under 2f out: kpt on same pce u.p* **25/1**	118
9	*nk*	**Winter (IRE)**22 6958 3-8-9 0 .... RyanMoore 8 (A P O'Brien, Ire) *w.w in midfield on rail: drvn along but n.m.r over 1 1/2f out: no imp appr fnl f: nvr trbld ldrs* **9/1**3	115
10	*¾*	**Zarak (FR)**91 4423 4-9-5 0 .... ChristopheSoumillon 18 (A De Royer-Dupre, France) *w.w towards rr: began to cl more than 2f out: effrt petered out fnl f: nvr beyond midfield* **28/1**	117+
11	*nk*	**One Foot In Heaven (IRE)**15 7177 5-9-5 0 .... JamesDoyle 11 (A De Royer-Dupre, France) *racd towards rr: rdn along over 2f out: styd on fr 1 1/2f out: run flattened out fnl 100yds* **80/1**	116+
12	*nk*	**Doha Dream (FR)**35 6499 4-9-5 0 .... GregoryBenoist 12 (A Fabre, France) *w.w in fnl trio: hdwy 1 1/2f out: kpt on past btn horses: nvr in contention* **200/1**	116+
13	*1 ½*	**Plumatic**15 7176 3-8-13 0 .... MaximeGuyon 14 (A Fabre, France) *settled in midfield: niggled along but n.m.r over 2f out: angled out and effrt u.p 1 1/2f out: wknd fnl f* **100/1**	114
14	*½*	**Seventh Heaven (IRE)**21 6972 4-9-2 0 .... PatSmullen 17 (A P O'Brien, Ire) *racd towards rr: rdn and no prog 2 1/2f out: nvr able to get involved* **50/1**	110+
15	*hd*	**Satono Diamond (JPN)**21 6983 4-9-5 0. Christophe-PatriceLemaire 13 (Yasutoshi Ikee, Japan) *w.w in fnl 3rd on outer: rdn and brief effrt 2f out: sn btn* **40/1**	112
16	*½*	**Satono Noblesse (JPN)**21 6983 7-9-5 0 .... YugaKawada 5 (Yasutoshi Ikee, Japan) *prom: outpcd and drvn 2f out: sn dropped away* **250/1**	111
17	*1*	**Capri (IRE)**15 7147 3-8-13 0 .... WayneLordan 15 (A P O'Brien, Ire) *scrubbed along early: sn settled towards rr of midfield: rdn towards rr over 2f out but no imp: wl hld fnl f* **20/1**	111
18	*20*	**Silverwave (FR)**21 6983 5-9-5 0 .... (h) Pierre-CharlesBoudot 16 (P Bary, France) *w.w in rr: lost tch fr 2f out: t.o* **150/1**	78+

2m 28.69s (-2.31) **Going Correction** +0.325s/f (Good)
WFA 3 from 4yo+ 6lb **18** Ran SP% **120.9**
Speed ratings: **120,118,117,116,115 115,115,115,114,114 114,114,113,112,112 112,111,98**
PARI-MUTUEL (all including 1 euro stake): WIN 1.80; PLACE 1.30, 3.40, 2.80; DF 17.50; SF 24.50.
Owner K Abdullah **Bred** Juddmonte Farms Ltd **Trained** Newmarket, Suffolk

L. DETTOR
PRIX

SEVEN

PRIX DE L'ARC DE TRIOMPHE

Longchamp, October 7, 2018

Previous spread: Enable and Frankie Dettori are all out to win the Prix de l'Arc de Triomphe at Longchamp in October 2018 from Sea Of Class and James Doyle

3.05 *Qatar Prix de l'Arc de Triomphe (Group 1) (3yo+ No Geldings) (Turf)* **ITV**
Winner £2,528,318.58 **1m4f**

£4424778.76 guaranteed **For** 3yo+ **Weights** 4yo+ colts 9-5; 4yo+ fillies 9-2; 3yo colts 8-13; 3yo fillies 8-9 **Entries** 95 **Confirmed** 19 **Penalty value 1st** £2,528,318.58 **2nd** £1,011,504.42 **3rd** £505,752.21 **4th** £252,654.87 **5th** £126,548.67

No. (Draw)	Form	Horse	Breeding	Trainer	Owner	Age	Wgt	Jockey	RPR
1 (18)	10-1132	**DEFOE** (IRE) 35	*gr c Dalakhani-Dulkashe*	**Roger Varian (GB)**	Sheikh Mohammed Obaid Al Maktoum	4	9-5	**Andrea Atzeni**	126
2 (7)	3-32343	**SALOUEN** (IRE) 42	*ch c Canford Cliffs-Gali Gal*	**Sylvester Kirk (GB)**	H Balasuriya	4	9-5	**Oisin Murphy**	127
3 (4)	6110-15	**CAPRI** (IRE) 21	*gr c Galileo-Dialafara*	**A P O'Brien (IRE)**	D Smith & Mrs J Magnier & M Tabor	4	9-5	**Donnacha O'Brien**	130
4 (10)	-242364	**WAY TO PARIS** 21	*gr h Champs Elysees-Grey Way*	**Antonio Marcialis (ITY)**	Paolo Ferrario	5	9-5	**Gerald Mosse**	123
5 (13)	4-51111	**WALDGEIST** 21	*ch c Galileo-Waldlerche*	**A Fabre**	Gestut Ammerland & Newsells Park	4	9-5	**Pierre-Charles Boudot**	131
6 (9)	-233643	**CLOTH OF STARS** (IRE) 21	*b h Sea The Stars-Strawberry Fledge*	**A Fabre**	Godolphin Snc	5	9-5	**Vincent Cheminaud**	128
7 (8)	12-1912	**TALISMANIC** 21	*b/br h Medaglia d'Oro-Magic Mission*	**A Fabre**	Godolphin Snc	5	9-5	**Mickael Barzalona**	127
8 (5)	70-4725	**TIBERIAN** (FR) 42	*b h Tiberius Caesar-Toamasina*	**Alain Couetil**	Aus Thoroghbred Bloodstock Ltd, H Volz Et Al	6	9-5	**William Buick**	124
9 (1)	92-1336	**CLINCHER** (JPN) 21	*b c Deep Sky-The Fates*	**Hiroshi Miyamoto (JPN)**	Koji Maeda	4	9-5	**Yutaka Take**	127
10 (6)	11111-1	**ENABLE** 29	*b f Nathaniel-Concentric*	**John Gosden (GB)**	K Abdullah	4	9-2	**Frankie Dettori**	138
11 (11)	121123	**NEUFBOSC** (FR) 21	*gr c Mastercraftsman-Nonsuch Way*	**Mme Pia Brandt**	Gerard Augustin-Normand	3	8-13	**Cristian Demuro**	123
12 (2)	13-1222	**PATASCOY** (FR) 53	*b c Wootton Bassett-Noble World*	**X Thomas-Demeaulte**	Roberto Cocheteux Tierno	3	8-13	**Olivier Peslier**	122
13 (14)	3291131	**KEW GARDENS** (IRE) 22	*b c Galileo-Chelsea Rose*	**A P O'Brien (IRE)**	D Smith & Mrs J Magnier & M Tabor	3	8-13	**Ryan Moore**	129
14 (19)	1-21135	**STUDY OF MAN** (IRE) 22	*b c Deep Impact-Second Happiness*	**P Bary**	Flaxman Stables Ireland Ltd	b3	8-13	**Stephane Pasquier**	123
15 (17)	303356	**LOUIS D'OR** (IRE) 21	*ch c Intello-Soudanaise*	**T Castanheira**	Camille Garnier	3	8-13	**Antoine Hamelin**	122
16 (12)	3361382	**HUNTING HORN** (IRE) 21	*b c Camelot-Mora Bai*	**A P O'Brien (IRE)**	Mrs John Magnier & Michael Tabor & Derrick Smith	3	8-13	**Seamie Heffernan**	124
17 (3)	-163567	**NELSON** (IRE) 22	*b c Frankel-Moonstone*	**A P O'Brien (IRE)**	Mrs J Magnier & M Tabor & D Smith	3	8-13	**Michael Hussey**	122
18 (16)	244-414	**MAGICAL** (IRE) 22	*b f Galileo-Halfway To Heaven*	**A P O'Brien (IRE)**	D Smith & Mrs J Magnier & M Tabor	3	8-9	**Wayne Lordan**	124
19 (15)	21111	**SEA OF CLASS** (IRE) 45	*ch f Sea The Stars-Holy Moon*	**William Haggas (GB)**	Sunderland Holding Inc	3	8-9	**James Doyle**	132

2017 (18 ran) **Enable** (2) John Gosden 3 8-9 10/11F Frankie Dettori RPR129

BETTING FORECAST: Evens Enable, 7-2 Sea Of Class, 7 Waldgeist, 10 Kew Gardens, 25 Capri, 33 Cloth Of Stars, Defoe, Neufbosc, Study Of Man, Talismanic, 40 Patascoy, 50 Clincher, Magical, Way To Paris, 66 Hunting Horn, 100 bar.

THE NEW YEAR started with Frankie Dettori visiting Enable in Newmarket in the middle of January. He went to Clarehaven Stables with the intention of sharing out a packet of Polo mints among the equine inhabitants. Enable got the lot.

Looking back on 2017, Dettori said: 'I was able to really enjoy the experience of winning the King George, Yorkshire Oaks and Arc on her because I knew how good she was after we won the Irish Oaks.

'I could have ridden her with one hand that day. She travels like no other horse I've ridden in my career.'

He described Enable's Arc triumph as 'nerve-racking but beautiful', adding: 'We had no doubt she should win, but the manner in which she did it was breathtaking.'

At the beginning of May Enable met with a setback and would not be out until August at the earliest.

Teddy Grimthorpe said: 'Enable has some filling in a knee and we are going to investigate it and then treat it or deal with it as advised.

'If it was a minor knock we might be saying that while she might not make the Coronation Cup she could still be back later in June, but with this we're going to allow plenty of time for it to hopefully settle down and then aim to get her rolling in August.

'The advice we have is that, given reasonable circumstances, she should be ready to run then as a preparation for the Prix de l'Arc de Triomphe.'

During the summer, the September Stakes at Kempton emerged as the likely starting point and in the lead-up to the race Dettori made a rare morning visit to the gallops to put Enable through her final workout.

Gosden said: 'Enable is very fresh in every sense of the word and we were pleased with what we saw this morning. It will be nice to get her back on track and the September Stakes falls just right as it's a month before the Arc.'

Enable was ready for her return to the track as David Milnes reported from Kempton:

Enable returns in style at Kempton with a three-and-a-half-length victory over Crystal Ocean in September 2018

Last season's spectacular Arc heroine Enable returned in style from an 11-month absence to leave King George runner-up Crystal Ocean in her wake and earn a quote of 9-4 to defend her crown at Longchamp on October 7. Enable, a five-time Group 1 winner last year, looked well up for it in the preliminaries and was full of it on the way to post, but that did not put off punters who backed her in to 8-15 (from 8-11) minutes before the off.

After the morning absence of pacemaker and stablemate Weekender, Frankie Dettori took the initiative on the Khalid Abdullah-owned four-year-old, who led the way at a decent clip from Crystal Ocean.

Turning for home, Dettori pushed the button at the two-furlong pole and his mount surged clear of Sir Michael Stoute's colt to score cosily by three and a half lengths, without the rider needing to resort to the whip.

Trainer John Gosden said: 'I was confident Enable would do that today as she's high class. That was a nice race for both horses if you're having a prep for an Arc and it was good to see Enable back, as it's been a long wait.

'She'll come on for that as she was only 80 per cent fit – 85 at a stretch – but she's in a good place mentally and she's enjoyed it. It's been very frustrating for her, as it has for us, especially when she's seen the other horses going out on the Heath.'

Gosden said of the second, who was giving Enable 8lb: 'I thought David Probert showed a lot of class by not leaning on her early, and fair play to him.'

Dettori was also impressed: 'That was awesome. I wasn't sure how fit she was as she's only being going a mile at home, but then she's

Enable and Frankie Dettori are led out on to the track at Kempton

trained by a master trainer. She got the job done and felt as good as ever. Bring on the Arc!'

Teddy Grimthorpe, racing manager to the winning owner, said: 'We came here wanting a good comeback and we got one.

'If it had turned into a ding-dong battle with Crystal Ocean and she lost she would still have gone to the Arc, but to see her return like that was very pleasing. It's great that after 11 months out she came here and still knows what it's all about.'

Probert, who was riding Crystal Ocean for the first time, said: 'I was happy enough down the back, but with the 5lb penalty it was hard to serve it up to Enable properly in the straight.'

RACING POST RATINGS VIEW – **PAUL CURTIS**

Enable looked as good as ever in making a stylish winning return to action in the September Stakes, making the most of a straightforward opportunity on paper but still returning a Racing Post Rating of 126+, close to her three-year-old best.

In receipt of 8lb from Crystal Ocean, Enable had 10lb in hand of the King George runner-up on adjusted RPRs and was entitled to win in such style. But to do so on her return from the best part of a year off strongly suggests she can at least repeat her three-year-old peak RPR of 129.

If that's the case then she'll take some beating in her bid for a repeat Arc success, as with her fillies' allowance the boys would need to run to an RPR of at least 133 to beat her, which looks highly unlikely.

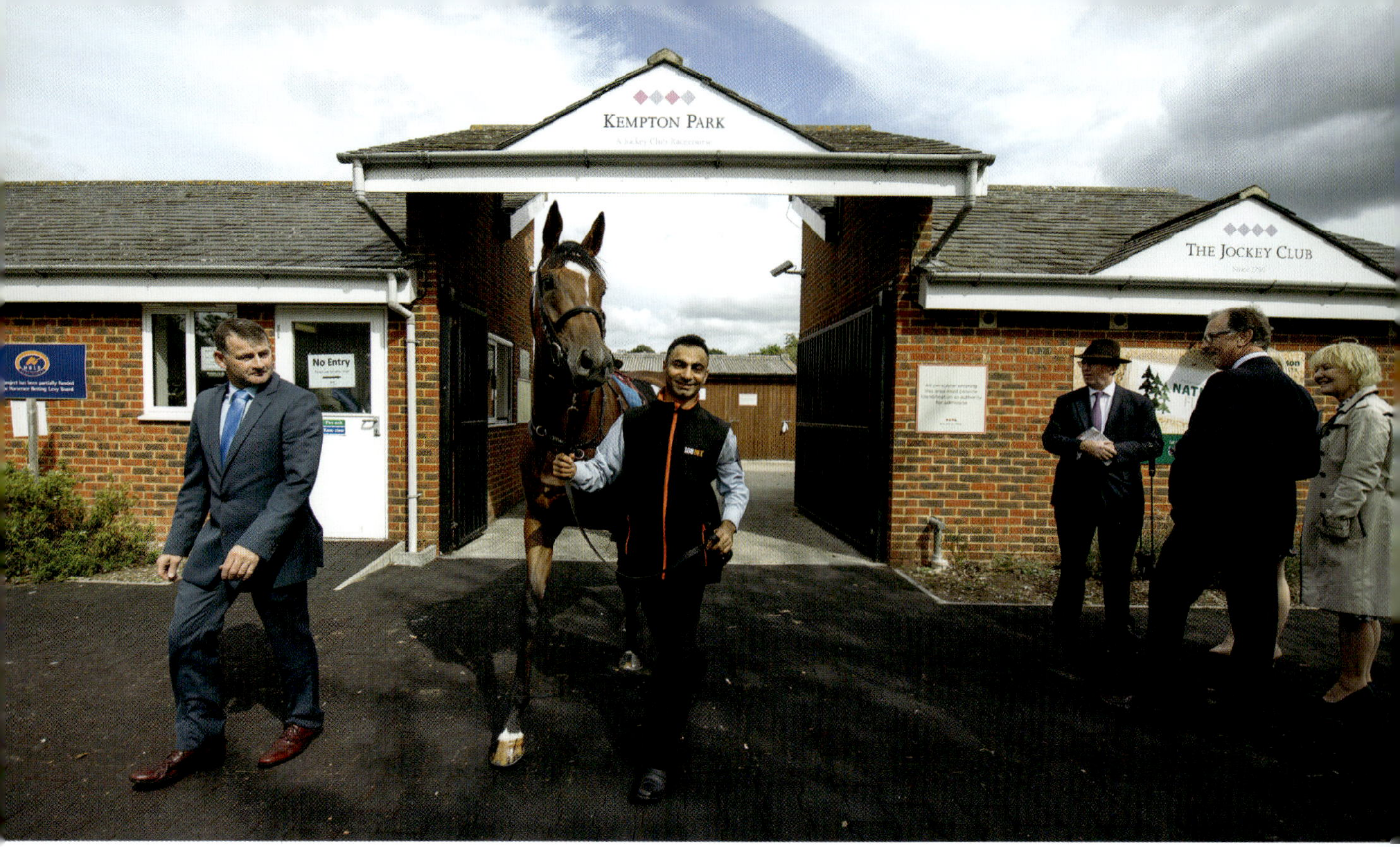

Enable and Imran Shahwani leave the racecourse stables at Kempton as connections watch on

Lee Mottershead was also at Kempton to see Enable's winning reappearance:

Once she was asked to quicken Enable did not hang around. Nor did her connections.

John Gosden was off to America, Teddy Grimthorpe was off to Ascot and Frankie Dettori was off home to Newmarket in the Gredleys' chopper. What took place was a mass exodus of Kempton, to such an extent you had to feel sorry for the nursery that came next.

This was a day that revolved around one race. In truth it revolved around one horse.

It is testament to the reputation and prowess of Enable that she completely overshadowed Crystal Ocean both before, during and after the best and most important Flat race staged here in more than three decades.

True, Crystal Ocean was seeking to concede 8lb to last year's imperious Arc heroine. Conversely, he arrived in the midst of a marvellous season, in which his latest King George second took him to a lofty BHA rating of 129. Yet punters pummelled Enable into 8-15 favouritism, seemingly certain she would see off her top-class rival – which Gosden made clear he had expected the glorious filly to do.

'I was confident she would do that, yeah,' he said just after Dettori has dismounted from his equine sweetheart and given her an adoring kiss that prompted the many racegoers around the paddock to go 'aaahhh' in unison.

Enable's jockey had needed to be only marginally less soppy during the race. Having sent his mount straight into the lead, he allowed her to amble through the first couple of furlongs. After looking between his legs before taking the home bend he requested a change of pace from his illustrious partner. He got one.

Crystal Ocean gave chase under David Probert but could not get close, Dettori needing no more than rhythmic waving of his whip to secure a wide-margin triumph.

Gosden had a date with an aircraft at Heathrow, from where he was flying out for the Keeneland sales, but even fighting against the clock he had time to eulogise about the now hot Arc favourite.

A worm's eye view as Enable and Frankie Dettori cruise to success at Kempton from Crystal Ocean

Before the injury that sidelined her until now he revealed her work had been exceptional, before comparing her mindset to those of Federer and Nadal.

'She was determined to come back, so it's all down to her and nothing to do with us,' he said. 'All our staff have worked very hard but she's a great person to deal with and really wanted to come back.'

Then, asked if this Group 3 success felt as good as a Group 1 victory, he added: 'To bring back the best mile-and-a-half filly you're ever likely to train in your life means an awful lot. There have been some long days.'

At this point. Grimthorpe, racing manager to owner Khalid Abdullah, intervened. 'The job is not yet done,' he said. Indeed it is not. It does, however, look much more likely to be done.

Most of those watching on the first Sunday of October will surely hope she does it. We have missed Enable this Flat season but absence really can make the heart grow fonder. The affection and admiration for her was obvious on a memorable day for all-weather racing and

Journalists gather round Frankie Dettori to get his view on Enable's winning return at Kempton

for Kempton, which will hopefully have many more such days over many more years.

Come the most special day in European Flat racing, Dettori could have the choice between stablemates Enable, Lah Ti Dar and Cracksman, although Gosden stressed good ground would be needed for the big boy to run.

He also dropped a very strong hint Dettori's choice has already been made when suggesting his number-one rider is nearly as fond of this champion as he is of his wife.

'Look, he loves this filly,' said Gosden. 'I told Catherine she's very lucky Enable has got four legs.'

Those legs, I'm pleased to report, still move extremely quickly.

Enable's achievements prompted Gosden to praise Khalid Abdullah for having the ambition that allowed Juddmonte Farms to produce one special filly in a long line of champions.

'Prince Khalid is a man who totally and completely understands his pedigrees and completely has a feel for his horses,' he explained. 'It's very hard indeed to create these families from nowhere, it takes years and years and years, and he's done it all, in terms of breeding and genetics, in such a short space of time.

'Everything now is so instantaneous in the way we live our lives, but his has been a work of passion, incredible diligence and care, almost playing God in a sense, while having to accept that a lot of it doesn't go right.

'It's an unparalleled achievement in that period of time, to create the sheer depth of quality he has, and Enable is simply a perfect example of what he has done.'

This was the perfect opportunity for Peter Thomas to chart the rise of the latest equine marvel from Prince Khalid's breeding powerhouse:

Were a Juddmonte Farms filly to be of a nervous disposition, she'd do well not to dwell too long on the roll of honour that accompanies the 41-year history of Prince Khalid Abdullah's global breeding empire. A short stroll through the Hall of Fame would be enough to engender humility at the very least, with an inferiority complex a distinct possibility.

There's no sign, however, that Enable has ever been overawed by the weight of expectation on her handsome brown shoulders – and why should she be? True enough, the litany of Group 1-winning homebreds is an awesome one, from the 1988 Sussex Stakes and QEII hero Warning to the mighty Frankel and Kingman, now exercising their potency at Banstead Manor Stud in Newmarket, not forgetting fillies of the calibre of Special Duty, Banks Hill and Wince.

But then Enable herself has the same blue blood coursing through her veins and has never looked anything other than a suitable heir to a great tradition.

Any doubts about her over-arching talent, caused by the one blot on her copybook – defeat at Newbury on her seasonal reappearance as a three-year-old – took no time at all to be dispelled, and in six bright and glorious months she emerged as not only a five-time Group 1 winner in her own right but, far more significantly for the grander scheme, also the 25th Classic winner to have emerged from Juddmonte and their 200th scorer at the highest level.

'She's testament to the many years and many generations of Juddmonte Farms, to the way they have nursed and created and continued to develop families,' acknowledges John Gosden, a trainer whose history with the green, pink and white goes back further than any other. 'It's an extraordinary achievement. I've trained for Prince Khalid since 1980 in America, so I'm probably the longest-surviving trainer, and I've seen it from the very beginning.'

And now he's nurturing the latest in an unbroken line of superstars. When Enable won the Prix de l'Arc de Triomphe at Chantilly last October, adding to her success in the King George, she was treading in the footsteps of Abdullah greats such as Dancing Brave. Her own sire Nathaniel had won the Ascot feature six years earlier, and his sire Galileo in 2001, and when allied to the formidable strength of such a proud Juddmonte family, this talent was unleashed in formidable fashion.

Enable is a fourth-generation exemplar of the longevity of Abdullah's investment of time, expertise and money in the breeding world. Her dam Concentric, a 2004-foaled daughter of Sadler's Wells, hails from a line begun when the Habitat mare Fleet Girl arrived in Juddmonte ownership as part of the asking price for Ferrans Stud in 1982; Fleet Girl's daughter Bourbon Girl was the product of a 1983 mating with another King George winner in Ile De Bourbon at Banstead Manor, even before the stud came under Juddmonte ownership; Bourbon Girl's daughter, the French Group 3 winner Apogee, by the 1978 Derby winner Shirley Heights, was in turn responsible for Concentric, who herself won in

Listed company at Chantilly but was destined to have an influence far beyond the racetrack, as the dam of Enable.

The long game at Juddmonte Farms isn't a flawless one, but in this 2014 bay filly with the big white star and the wonky blaze, it hit the jackpot.

When Gosden took delivery of her he was impressed by her physical presence, although she was always going to be the work of months rather than weeks.

'She had a very strong body and a great outlook and was always very forward-going and positive,' he recalls. 'She then grew a great deal, filled out her frame and took her time, hence she didn't run well into the backend of the year.

'She straight away showed a level of ability in winning her maiden at Newcastle [beating Lucy Wadham's Gallifrey by three and three-quarter lengths at the positively Santa Clausian odds of 7-2], but when she came back the next April it was very difficult at the time, because we didn't have novice races, so we were forced to run in a colts' conditions race and she got caught in a little pocket that day and was beaten by a stablemate, a nice filly of Mr Abdullah's who went on to win the Musidora.'

John Gosden says Enable is a testament to the Juddmonte Farms operation

For those with a narrow outlook, this third place at Newbury at the hands of her fellow Juddmonte runner Shutter Speed and Raheen House may have seemed a stunning blow to Enable's heady reputation, but those closest to her were satisfied enough with her efforts over a barely adequate ten furlongs to send her straight to the Cheshire Oaks.

On the Roodee, under the educational urgings of Frankie Dettori, she beat Coolmore's even-money favourite Alluringly by an eased-down length and three-quarters over half a furlong short of a mile and a half, thus beginning the process of subjugating the massed ranks of middle-distance fillies.

Teddy Grimthorpe, racing manager to Abdullah, immediately nominated Epsom as the filly's next port of call. It was hardly a shock, given Enable's stamina profile and her generous way of going about her job. Dettori announced he had always felt she was travelling in her comfort zone, quickening when asked and practically begging for her stab at a Classic.

'She really enjoyed her racing and training, which made it a pleasure to train her,' confirms Gosden. 'She was always there for you in every way and she and Frankie built up a great affinity, which was

Enable canters up Warren Hill in the hands of groom Imran Shahwani in September 2018

a major asset, and from then on she dominated her division and beyond.'

If the thoroughbred racehorse exists, as it is said to, because of the winning post of the Derby, then that famed piece of wood is no less a measure of the excellence of a breed-enhancing filly when it signals the finish of the Oaks. Enable's first Group 1 mission was thus to assert her superiority over her own sex, and in this she succeeded at the first attempt.

With Dettori at ease in his Classic playground, she demolished a passably strong field, leaving previous and subsequent Group 1 winner Rhododendron trailing her at a respectful five lengths. She outstayed the non-stayers and outspeeded the stayers, leaving the path all of a sudden blindingly clear for a season of triumph. The Leger was mooted, along with the King George, but one thing was for certain: never again would punters let her start at these dismissive odds of 6-1. Epsom was the start of a magnificent summer run, sometimes little more than a stroll, that encompassed five victories in the top grade. The Irish Oaks at the Curragh was landed by more than five lengths from Coolmore's

Enable walks back to John Gosden's Clarehaven Stables after working on Warren Hill

Rain Goddess, with Dettori asking the 2-5 shot to lengthen more than two furlongs from home off a modest pace and gallop her field into supplication.

Gosden instantly floated the idea of taking on the colts. 'She's probably the best we've got, exceptionally good,' he reasoned. 'She's in the King George in two weeks and we'll see what we think.'

With time to reflect, the Juddmonte camp might have been forgiven for taking a long, hard look at the Ascot field and deciding to follow an easier route to the autumn. There were hard-baked colts waiting for her there – the Eclipse winner Ulysses, the Great Voltigeur and Hardwicke star Idaho and the reigning champion Highland Reel, not to mention her Irish Derby-winning stablemate Jack Hobbs – but she arrived with an aura of confidence about her and dispatched those rivals and more with a performance that proved not only her predominance but also her versatility and grit, in torrential rain on a surface quickly veering towards quagmire.

Four and a half lengths was her mud-spattered margin of superiority over Ulysses, prompting Gosden to say: 'She can handle anything.'

It was a fact that crystallised the remainder of the season, with rain-softened ground in France plainly holding no fears for the filly, and only a prep race at York to take care of in between times.

Having dealt summarily with the best colts, Enable stepped back into the ring on the Knavesmire against her own sex and settled the race from flagfall, making her own running, just in case, and pulling five lengths clear of her Ribblesdale-winning stablemate Coronet and Breeders' Cup heroine Queen's Trust.

Dettori spoke of 'five weeks of sleepless nights' before Chantilly, but in his mind can have resided few doubts about her readiness for the test. 'I would prefer to have a lead but Enable is sensible enough to make the running and that's another option we've got if we go to an Arc and it's a small field – we've got that weapon in our armoury,' he gushed.

'She's a stayer with a turn of foot and she's uncomplicated. If you try to keep up with her, she'll break your lungs. I said to John [Gosden] that if something had sniffed her backside [at York] she would have taken off, but she was too far clear.'

It may not have been the effusive Dettori's most savoury assessment, but here was a seasoned jockey who knew he was aboard a horse with no discernible weakness, and although he didn't have to resort to making his own running in the Arc, he was able to ride the race with the security of his partner's impenetrable tactical shield.

In truth, there was nothing for Enable or her rider to be frightened of in France. She started at odds-on because she had already

Enable follows three stablemates back to Clarehaven Stables after her latest workout

seen off one of her main market rivals, the 126-rated Ulysses, and seemed to have little to fear from the others, including the Gold Cup winner Order Of St George and the Aidan O'Brien-trained Winter, who received all the same allowances as her fellow three-year-old filly.

Naturally, Coolmore were mob-handed and there were the usual collection of wildcards from Europe and Japan, but Dettori held all the aces on the rain-softened ground and knew when to play them.

On this occasion he sat handy from the start, tracking Idaho and Order Of St George, looking round eagle-eyed for potential spoilers. On the final turn he was still on the heels of the leaders with his mount travelling eagerly but under restraint, until with more than two furlongs to run he angled her to the outside and unleashed an unanswerable surge that tore the field to shreds.

Cloth Of Stars stayed on gamely to be second by two and a half lengths, with Ulysses third, but this was a case of Enable first, the rest of the world nowhere. She had capped a wondrous campaign with her most spectacular win, and the superlatives queued up to be thrown her way.

'She is very special and has amazing ability,' said Gosden, although this was something we knew already. 'She showed us at home she was in the zone. She was looking well, eating well, still had her summer coat and she enjoys her work. She gave us every sign she was ready to run a race like that.'

Here was a filly whose pedigree, constitution, physical prowess and mental attitude combined to produce the near perfect storm of a season, and although injury kept her off the track between that memorable October day and her less exalted reappearance win at Kempton 11 months later, Gosden issued an assessment that must have struck dread into the hearts of her rivals at Longchamp this year.

'She's always been a very striking filly, beautiful and a great walker, very powerful and with a great outlook. She's filled that frame out, won nicely on her reappearance and has had the perfect prep, coming fresh to the Arc, which at this stage is probably not a bad thing.'

The day before the Arc, Gosden revealed that the Breeders' Cup at Churchill Downs at the start of November was under consideration if Enable came through Longchamp in good shape.

1
L'ARC
ARC DE

Previous spread: Enable and Frankie Dettori (left) lead the way as Sea Of Class and James Doyle (second right) cut through the pack to set up a thrilling climax to the Arc at Longchamp in October 2018

Frankie Dettori is all smiles after Enable clings on to win the Arc from Sea Of Class (second right)

With the Arc draw having been kind – stall six left her close to the inside rail – there were plenty of reasons for connections to be excited.

David Jennings was at Longchamp to see Enable claim back-to-back Arcs:

The perfect place. The perfect race. The perfect result. The perfect racehorse. This was an Arc gift-wrapped with greatness.

Back home at Longchamp and in front of a new €145 million glitzy grandstand, the pressure was on the world's most prestigious Flat race to produce something special. What we got was something so special that replays will be shown over and over again and no-one will ever get sick of seeing it. It was an Arc for the ages.

Enable defended her crown in the most intoxicating of circumstances but 2018 was light years away from 2017 in every possible way.

Last year's stunning success, achieved with the ease of a filly vastly superior to her peers, arrived at the end of a gruelling seven-race

campaign that saw her mop up three Oaks and a King George along the way.

This Arc was ground out on the back of an all-weather spin around Kempton only 29 days earlier. No previous Arc winner had got the job done on the back of just one run in the that calendar year, but this is no ordinary filly. This is a filly whose ability is outweighed only by her attitude.

'It's been a nightmare year, I'm feeling a deep sense of relief – the elation will come later,' admitted a visibly relieved trainer John Gosden, later to be hailed a genius by Frankie Dettori. And rightly so.

'It's absolutely massive for the filly,' he continued. 'It's not easy when they go lame and they're off for a long time. She has such a fantastic mind. It's like a manager with a top player who always gives you 100 per cent. You can build your team around her.

'You're not meant to come into the Arc after one run on the all-weather. I had a slight hiccup between Kempton and here, which wasn't ideal either. She had a temperature and missed a piece of work, and the way the race was run tested her fitness. The last 100 metres were an eternity for me, the jockey and the horse.'

Those thrilling final 100 metres might have felt like an eternity for Gosden but they flew by in the blink of an eye for William Haggas and James Doyle as the line came a stride, or two at most, too early for Sea Of Class.

The daughter of Sea The Stars, who this year followed a similar path to Enable in 2017 by winning the Irish and Yorkshire Oaks, trailed the 19-runner pack on the home turn but arrived with her customary late burst, which ended an agonising short neck away from a share of victory.

How fitting to see two top-class fillies fight out the finish to a race which has been dominated by females in recent years. The colts have not been able to cope of late, with only Golden Horn managing to get the boys on the roll of honour in the last eight years. Fillies have won eight out of the last 11 Arcs, going back to Zarkava.

One boy who can't keep away from the roll of honour is Dettori. This was his sixth Arc success, two more than any other rider has managed, and you sense it was his most fulfilling of all.

'I can't believe it, I'm actually lost for words,' said Dettori.

Luckily for us all he soon found quite a few more to put the performance into context.

Frankie Dettori shows his delight after claiming a sixth Arc on Enable

'She wasn't the Enable of last year but she has got the job done and that's all that matters,' he said. 'I said beforehand, "Let's try to win the Arc and it doesn't have to be by five lengths".

'This showed what a genius John Gosden is. He's won the Arc with a filly who hadn't run in 11 months. Two Arcs for the same horse at two different racetracks. I don't think that will ever be done again.'

Gosden deflected all the praise away from Dettori, and indeed himself, and urged racing fans to realise the importance of owner-breeder Prince Khalid Abdullah.

He said: 'It's not about me, it's about the owner-breeder and the filly. Without owner-breeders like Prince Khalid Abdullah this game is dead.'

Dettori also helps keep the game alive more than most, and he bounced from interview to interview with as much enthusiasm as ever. He's 47, supposedly. Someone check his birth certificate.

'There was almighty pressure on all of us,' he admitted. 'The world was behind me. Everybody wanted her to win. I wasn't riding a 10-1 shot, I was riding the favourite in the most famous race in the world. I'm looking forward to watching the replay.'

So are we, Frankie. So are we.

Tom Kerr watched a nerve-racking finish:

A tale of two fillies unfolded in Paris as reigning Arc champion Enable successfully defended her crown at Longchamp in the most nerve-shredding of circumstances, holding off the late, lunging charge of Sea Of Class to win by a short neck and join the ranks of Europe's great racehorses.

Just eight horses have won the Arc twice in nigh on a century and none has done it, as Enable did, off an injury-blighted campaign that began only one month earlier.

It was a triumph for her rider Frankie Dettori, her trainer John Gosden and her owner-breeder Khalid Abdullah, whose racing manager Teddy Grimthorpe accurately described Enable as 'the ultimate thoroughbred' and left open the tantalising possibility she could bid for a record-breaking third Arc victory next year.

Yet she came within desperate inches of being toppled by the brilliant Sea Of Class, who weaved through the field in game pursuit of Enable and came so close to glory that the devastation was wrought plain on jockey James Doyle's face when he made his way back into the winner's enclosure to richly deserved applause.

It was the cruellest of outcomes for Sea Of Class and her connections, yet it would have been even more agonising if Enable had been pipped to the post after summoning from a Mariana Trench of courage one of the bravest performances this storied racecourse has ever seen.

A knee injury had kept her off the track through the spring and summer and only in September, almost a month to the day before the Arc, did she return with an easy victory on the all-weather surface of Kempton.

It was cutting things fine, to put it mildly, although memories of her stunning three-year-old campaign, which culminated in a scintillating Arc success at its temporary home of Chantilly, meant she was sent off an odds-on favourite at the redeveloped Longchamp.

Sea Of Class, by contrast, had the perfect run to Paris, marching through her season to an ever-strengthening beat. She won the Irish

L. DETTORI
10
J. DOYLE

Previous spread: There's only a short neck in it as Enable and Frankie Dettori hold on from the fast-finishing Sea Of Class

Above: Enable and Frankie Dettori return to the Longchamp winner's enclosure after the Arc

Oaks under an ice-cold ride by Doyle, then eviscerated her rivals in the Yorkshire Oaks in August.

A late foal and a late starter on the racecourse, she was palpably improving with each outing and if anyone was to topple Enable, it would surely be her.

Yet Sea Of Class had her own hurdle to overcome. Drawn wide in 15 and a habitual hold-up horse, she faced having to come through the entire Arc field to chase down the leaders. It was a challenge she rose to in awesome fashion, even if, in the end, her effort came up a soupcon short of victory.

While Enable, drawn kindly, was positioned ideally just behind the front-runners by Dettori, Sea Of Class was still sitting dead last as the field entered the false straight. From there Doyle launched her on her audacious assault, advancing swiftly through the field and – remarkably – avoiding all but the most inconsequential of traffic bumps.

A furlong and a half out Doyle had to switch left to round his good friend William Buick, riding Tiberian, but Sea Of Class manoeuvred and accelerated away beautifully. From there, she was in the clear and bearing down on Enable.

Yet the favourite had got first run. 'We passed the 300-metre mark and I said, "Come on girl, let's go" and the usual trademark turn of foot was there,' said Dettori. It may not have been as spectacular as last year, when Enable took off like a rocket from Cape Canaveral, but it was no less devastating, taking the filly two lengths clear of the chasing pack.

It looked for all the world to be over with just 100 metres to run, but then the tank emptied beneath Dettori, his brave girl suddenly all out like a boxer swaying on heels, and Sea Of Class closing, closing, closing, until the pair flashed by the line, almost nothing in it, a heart-stopping finish to a sensational contest.

For all that the heart ached for Sea Of Class, it soared for Enable, not just a magnificent winner once more but one who overcame adversity and summoned hitherto unknown reserves to secure victory.

The motto of Paris is 'Elle est battue par les flots, mais ne sombre pas', which translates as 'She is tossed by the waves, but does not sink' – a defiant rallying cry that could just as easily be applied to the filly who secured racing immortality before the Eiffel Tower.

Arc day last year at Chantilly was a blessed one for the invaders from across the Channel, British and Irish trained horses carrying off all six Group 1s, and back at Longchamp they fared little worse.

As well as the Arc, the Lagardere (Royal Marine for Saeed bin Suroor), the Opera (Wild Illusion for Charlie Appleby), Abbaye (Mabs Cross for Michael Dods) all went to the raiders.

And the near-rout of the French was capped in the Foret, when Sea Of Class's trainer William Haggas achieved some modest consolation with One Master.

Fine wins all, but none could come close to upstaging a sensational finale to an Arc that was either the best of times or the worst of times, depending on which of two fantastic flying fillies you had tied your colours to.

With Europe conquered for a second time it was time to head west to America.

RACING POST RATINGS VIEW – **SAM WALKER**

Enable ran below her best but was still good enough to etch her name in history with a second victory in the Prix de l'Arc de Triomphe.

John Gosden said we had not seen her at her peak and the figures concur, as she earned a Racing Post Rating of 122 for her second Arc success – 7lb below the mark she received last year.

She had an interrupted preparation, which became evident in the final 100 yards, where she quickly went from three lengths up and powering away from the third and fourth to fading and just doing enough to hold on.

Sea Of Class (121) thundered home from off the pace and just failed to pick up the champ, losing out by a short neck.

Cloth Of Stars (123) finished a further three-quarters of a length away in third, getting closer to the winner this time round than when second in the race last year.

The winner's rating of 122 is well below standard for an Arc but that is partly a result of this being the tightest finish to the race for 20 years, with less than seven lengths covering the first 12 horses – and within that group there are plenty who Enable at her best would have beaten by further.

Enable earned a higher rating than this when beating Crystal Ocean in the September Stakes on her previous start, so this performance is hardly a signal of her decline. We can put this down to her having an off day and still being too good.

8026a **QATAR PRIX DE L'ARC DE TRIOMPHE (GROUP 1) (3YO+ NO GELDINGS) (TURF)** **1m 4f**

3:05 3-Y-O+ **£2,528,318** (£1,011,504; £505,752; £252,654; £126,548)

			RPR
1		**Enable**[29] 7065 4-9-2 0.. FrankieDettori 6 (John Gosden) *in tch: trckd ldrs gng wl 2f out: rdn under 2f out: led 1 1/2f out: drvn fnl 100yds: pressed and began to weaken clsng stages: jst hld on* **1/1**[1]	122
2	*snk*	**Sea Of Class (IRE)**[45] 6457 3-8-9 0................................ JamesDoyle 15 (William Haggas) *hld up in rr: hdwy fr 2 1/2f out: rdn 2f out: nt clr run and swtchd 1 1/2f out: drvn over 1f out: styd on strly fnl f: pressed wnr clsng stages: jst hld* **6/1**[2]	121
3	*3/4*	**Cloth Of Stars (IRE)**[21] 7350 5-9-5 0.................... VincentCheminaud 9 (A Fabre, France) *hld up towards rr of midfield: hdwy appr 2f out: rdn 2f out: chsd ldrs ent fnl f: kpt on wl: nt able to chal* **28/1**	123
4	*3/4*	**Waldgeist**[21] 7350 4-9-5 0.................................. Pierre-CharlesBoudot 13 (A Fabre, France) *hld up towards rr of midfield: pushed along and hdwy fr 2 1/2f out: nt clr run under 2f out: rdn and styd on fr 1 1/2f out* **6/1**[2]	121
5	*1 1/2*	**Capri (IRE)**[21] 7350 4-9-5 0... DonnachaO'Brien 4 (A P O'Brien, Ire) *chsd ldr: rdn 2 1/2f out: led under 2f out: hdd 1 1/2f out: no ex fnl f* **25/1**	119
6	*1/2*	**Salouen (IRE)**[42] 6607 4-9-5 0... OisinMurphy 7 (Sylvester Kirk) *racd keenly in midfield on inner: rdn and kpt on wl fr 2 1/2f out: nt clr run 125yds out* **80/1**	118
7	*nk*	**Kew Gardens (IRE)**[22] 7293 3-8-13 0............................. RyanMoore 14 (A P O'Brien, Ire) *hld up towards rr: rdn and stdy hdwy fr 2 1/2f out: styd on ins fnl f: nrst fin* **8/1**[3]	119
8	*nk*	**Nelson (IRE)**[22] 7293 3-8-13 0..................................... MichaelHussey 3 (A P O'Brien, Ire) *led: rdn under 3f out: hdd under 2f out: wknd fnl f* **100/1**	118
9	*snk*	**Study Of Man (IRE)**[22] 7318 3-8-13 0..............(b[1]) StephanePasquier 19 (P Bary, France) *midfield on outer: rdn 2 1/2f out: drvn and sme hdwy fr under 2f out: wknd steadily fnl f* **40/1**	118
10	*3/4*	**Magical (IRE)**[22] 7316 3-8-9 0....................................... WayneLordan 16 (A P O'Brien, Ire) *hld up in rr: rdn 3f out: kpt on steadily on wd outside fr 2f out: n.d* **40/1**	113
11	*1/2*	**Way To Paris**[21] 7350 5-9-5 0.. GeraldMosse 10 (Antonio Marcialis, Italy) *hld up towards rr: rdn and kpt on steadily on inner fr 2 1/2f out: n.d* **150/1**	115
12	*3/4*	**Tiberian (FR)**[42] 6607 6-9-5 0.. WilliamBuick 5 (Alain Couetil, France) *in tch in midfield: rdn 2 1/2f out: effrt 1 1/2f out: wknd qckly 1f out* **200/1**	114
13	*4 1/2*	**Talismanic**[21] 7350 5-9-5 0... MickaelBarzalona 8 (A Fabre, France) *towards rr of midfield: rdn 2f out: sme hdwy fr 1 1/2f out: wknd ins fnl f* **25/1**	107
14	*snk*	**Patascoy (FR)**[53] 6175 3-8-13 0...................................... OlivierPeslier 2 (X Thomas-Demeaulte, France) *midfield: rdn 2 1/2f out: wknd fr under 2f out* **40/1**	107
15	*1/2*	**Defoe (IRE)**[35] 6844 4-9-5 0... AndreaAtzeni 18 (Roger Varian) *racd alone on wd outside first 3f: trckd ldrs whn joining main gp: rdn over 3f out: wknd over 2f out* **40/1**	106
16	*4 1/2*	**Hunting Horn (IRE)**[21] 7351 3-8-13 0..................... SeamieHeffernan 12 (A P O'Brien, Ire) *in tch in midfield on outer: rdn under 3f out: wknd 1 1/2f out* **40/1**	99
17	*2*	**Clincher (JPN)**[21] 7350 4-9-5 0.. YutakaTake 1 (Hiroshi Miyamoto, Japan) *in tch: rdn and unable qck 2f out: lost pl qckly 1 1/2f out* **100/1**	95
18	*3 1/2*	**Neufbosc (FR)**[21] 7351 3-8-13 0................................ CristianDemuro 11 (Mme Pia Brandt, France) *a towards rr* **40/1**	91
19	*dist*	**Louis D'Or (IRE)**[21] 7351 3-8-13 0............................ AntoineHamelin 17 (T Castanheira, France) *a in rr: t.o fr 2f out* **200/1**	

2m 29.24s (-1.16) **Going Correction** +0.375s/f (Good)
WFA 3 from 4yo+ 6lb **19** Ran SP% **120.3**
Speed ratings: **118,117,117,116,115 115,115,115,115,114 114,113,110,110,110 107,105,103,**
PARI-MUTUEL (all including 1 euro stake): WIN 2.00 PLACE 1.50, 2.00, 5.40 DF 5.70 SF 8.80.
Owner K Abdullah **Bred** Juddmonte Farms Ltd **Trained** Newmarket, Suffolk

EIGHT

BREEDERS' CUP TURF

Churchill Downs,
November 3, 2018

2
ONGINES
ENABLE

Previous spread: Frankie Dettori looks to the heavens after Enable's victory in the Breeders' Cup Turf at Churchill Downs in November 2018

8.56 *Longines Breeders' Cup Turf (Grade 1) (3yo+) (Turf)* **ATR**
Winner £1,629,629.63 **1m4f**

£2725925.93 guaranteed **For** 3yo+ **Penalty value 1st** £1,629,629.63 **2nd** £503,703.70 **3rd** £266,666.67 **4th** £148,148.15 **5th** £88,888.89 **6th** £29,629.63

2-19120 **1** (1) **TALISMANIC** 27 — 5 9-0
b/br h Medaglia d'Oro-Magic Mission — **Mickael Barzalona**
A Fabre (FR) Godolphin Snc — (132)

1111-11 **2** (2) **ENABLE** 27 — 4 8-11
b f Nathaniel-Concentric — **Frankie Dettori**
John Gosden (GB) K Abdullah — (139)

358121 **3** (3) **CHANNEL MAKER (CAN)** 35 — b 4 9-0
ch g English Channel-In Return — **Jose L Ortiz**
William Mott Wachtel Stable, Gary Barber Et Al — (132)

11-1612 **4** (4) **ROBERT BRUCE (CHI)** 35 — 4 9-0
b/br c Fast Company-Lady Pelusa — **Irad Ortiz Jr**
Chad C Brown Convento Viejo Llc — (129)

4-41401 **5** (5) **MAGICAL (IRE)** 14 — 3 8-7
b f Galileo-Halfway To Heaven — **Ryan Moore**
A P O'Brien (IRE) D Smith & Mrs J Magnier & M Tabor — (133)

244112 **6** (6) **ARKLOW (USA)** 16 — 4 9-0
b c Arch-Unbridled Empire — **Florent Geroux**
Brad H Cox Donegal Racing, Joseph Bulger & Peter Coneway — (122)

76-6111 **7** (7) **GLORIOUS EMPIRE (IRE)** 70 — 7 9-0
br g Holy Roman Emperor-Humble And Proud — **Julien R Leparoux**
James Lawrence II Matthew Schera — (126)

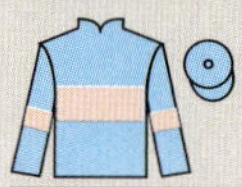
1480-11 **8** (8) **LIAM THE CHARMER (USA)** 34 — b 5 9-0
b/br g Smart Strike-Charm The Giant — **Tyler Gaffalione**
Michael McCarthy Madaket Stables Llc — (123)

277512 **9** (9) **QUARTETO DE CORDAS (BRZ)** 91 — 4 9-0
b c Rock Of Gibraltar-New Hampshire — **Brian Joseph Hernandez Jr**
Ian Wilkes Elite Performance Stable — (119)

113642 **10** (10) **HI HAPPY (ARG)** 26 — 6 9-0
ch h Pure Prize-Historia — **Luis Saez**
Todd Pletcher La Providencia — (126)

422363 **11** (11) **SADLER'S JOY (USA)** 35 — 5 9-0
ch h Kitten's Joy-Dynaire — **Javier Castellano**
Thomas Albertrani Woodslane Farm — (128)

511114 **12** (12) **WALDGEIST** 27 — 4 9-0
ch c Galileo-Waldlerche — **Pierre-Charles Boudot**
A Fabre (FR) Gestut Ammerland & Newsells Park — (135)

3613820 **13** (13) **HUNTING HORN (IRE)** 27 — 3 8-10
b c Camelot-Mora Bai — **Wayne Lordan**
A P O'Brien (IRE) Mrs J Magnier & M Tabor & D Smith — (128)

2017 (13 ran) **Talismanic** (1) A Fabre 4 9-0 14/1 Mickael Barzalona RPR118

BETTING FORECAST: 4-7 Enable, 6 Magical, Waldgeist, 14 Channel Maker, Talismanic, 20 Robert Bruce, 25 Glorious Empire, 40 Hunting Horn, 66 bar.

TEN DAYS AFTER the Arc Teddy Grimthorpe said the Breeders' Cup was a 'logical progression' for Enable as she had come out of the race in such good shape.

Eight previous Arc winners had tried and failed in their attempts to follow up in the Breeders' Cup, including Dancing Brave, Sakhee and the John Gosden-trained Golden Horn, but as Grimthorpe pointed out Enable had only had two runs in 2018.

Gosden added: 'She comes here relatively fresh after two runs and we'd be hopeful of a big run. But when you're shipping that far you don't go there full of confidence until you know how the horse has travelled.'

Enable enhanced her reputation further at Churchill Downs as Richard Forristal explained:

Enable was the one champion whose impenetrable reputation would have survived a defeat but we all wanted Enable to enhance her legacy in the Turf by becoming the first Arc winner to follow up at the same year's Breeders' Cup.

Frankie Dettori and Enable in action on the turf track at Churchill Downs in preparation for their Breeders' Cup bid

Where Dancing Brave first failed for Khalid Abdullah in 1986, she triumphed in glorious fashion, defying first being tightened up by Hunting Horn and then being coerced wide by Magical. She and Magical then settled down for an epic joust.

It was a yawning nine lengths back to Sadler's Joy in third, so Magical deserves credit too, but this was Enable's piece de resistance.

At the end of November it was revealed that Enable would stay in training as a five-year-old and would target an unprecedented third win in the Arc.

Grimthorpe said: 'I think Prince Khalid wanted to sit back and reflect and enjoy what she has done before coming to any decision. He didn't want to rush into anything. She only ran once as a two-year-old, had a full three-year-old season and only ran three times this year, so she doesn't have loads of miles on the clock.'

Abdullah has a long-standing affinity with the Arc and Grimthorpe added: 'It's clearly one of the great races of the world and obviously Prince Khalid is now joint-leading owner in terms of number of wins [six, with Marcel Boussac].

'If he were to take the record outright with the first three-time winner of the race, that would be something.'

In December Katherine Fidler caught up with Dettori in Hong Kong to reflect on an incredible year:

John Gosden accompanies Enable and Frankie Dettori after the filly's exercise on the turf track at Churchill Downs

Frankie Dettori has had a good year; a very good year. Simultaneously stating the obvious and an understatement that may be, but when talking about the face of the sport we need that face to be sporting its trademark smile that is recognised around the world. And there has been plenty to smile about in 2018.

A second Arc on Enable; the £1 million stayers' bonus courtesy of Stradivarius; another Champion Stakes with Cracksman; one for next year in Too Darn Hot. The list goes on – yet swap Enable for Ouija Board, Stradivarius for Sixties Icon, Too Darn Hot for Authorized and we could still be talking about the same jockey, different year.

Last season may have been the kind many can only dream of, but for Dettori it was very much a case of business as usual – with some extra highlights thrown in.

The Italian, who moved to Newmarket aged just 14, has been one of the most successful and consistent riders in the sport since becoming the first teenager since Lester Piggott to ride a century in 1990. Yet in his early years he didn't always see himself getting to where he is today.

'Believe it or not, I was quite conservative and shy when I was young,' Dettori says. 'Obviously my father [Gianfranco] was a big challenge for me, champion jockey 13 times – I never thought I'd get anywhere near him, I was happy just to try to make a living out of it. When I first started I didn't really have that much ambition. Then I realised I wasn't too bad at it.'

Those who have grown up with his flying dismounts, *Question Of Sport* appearances and ebullient post-race interviews may struggle to believe he was ever conservative or shy because to the outside world he looks to be living the life he was always meant to.

'The job sucked me into it, then it all snowballed out of control. I got addicted to the success, then wanted more and more winners, and the passion and adrenaline that comes with it all.'

As Dettori got more out of racing he put two-fold back in, reaping rewards as big-race wins and a bigger-name contract came his way. A first century, a retainer with Godolphin, a first Classic, first Arc, his 'Magnificent Seven' – the day that pushed him out of the racing bubble. There have been downs along with the ups, but he has bounced back from each one – ultimately to racing's benefit.

Now thanks to Enable, Cracksman and company he is soaring higher than ever and today, a few days before his 48th birthday, he will be crowned Longines World's Best Jockey for the second time. The acco-

2
DETTORI

CAL

Previous spread: Frankie Dettori punches the air as Enable holds on from Magical and Ryan Moore in a thrilling finale to the Breeders' Cup Turf

lade is a reminder that, in our world, his face is recognised in any country where fast horses, green turf and white rails come together.

'Racing has become much more global since I started out,' he says, asked to reflect on the sport's biggest change during his time in the saddle. 'Back then, we didn't really know what Hong Kong or Australian racing was, it was only from the early 90s we started travelling a bit.'

In the decades since, Dettori has won big prizes in every major racing jurisdiction, first in the Godolphin blue and now atop the seemingly inexhaustible string of top talent emerging from John Gosden's yard, headed by dual Arc winner Enable. The four-year-old kept her fans on tenterhooks for most of the season while recovering from injury, but promptly showed she had lost not one iota of talent.

'Her injury wasn't that serious, but it needed time to heal – it was a long process,' says Dettori. 'Of course I couldn't wait for her to come back.

'I probably rode her twice a week for three or four weeks before her first race [the September Stakes], got her to a point where I thought she was pretty fit. It was a four-horse race and I was able to dominate, went pretty slowly and she won – that was three weeks before the Arc.

'I rode her at Longchamp and it turns out she was probably at about 95 [per cent] – that extra five, when you haven't got it and they stop, it's pretty scary. Anyway, we got away with it!' Rarely would the Prix de l'Arc de Triomphe serve as a prep race, but in Enable's case it was the perfect stepping stone for the Breeders' Cup Turf, which the pair won less than a month later – and one half of a double for Dettori, who also took the Mile on Expert Eye.

After the self-proclaimed world championships in the US, racing moves on to Australia for the Melbourne Cup, then Japan, and finally Hong Kong. Jet lag seems a fair price for living the life of a top jockey, with less time in business class spent studying than you might think.

'More or less [our rules are] pretty in sync with everyone,' says Dettori. 'Obviously because in Australia the carnivals are more spread out the suspensions and fines are greater than anywhere else, but more or less we're speaking the same language.'

Less welcome is the parity between racing nations regarding the declining numbers speaking the language of racing. Not those pushing against the traditional and occasionally labyrinthine terminology, but against the sport itself – with one major flashpoint being the whip.

'I think the whip is essential, but we have to monitor the situation, we always have to be in touch with people who don't know too much about racing,' says Dettori.

'We have to keep up with the times.

The old days, with rock-hard crops [whips], that's all in the past, but you still have people who want to ban the whip – so in every jurisdiction it's a topic of conversation, and we need to ensure a good perception by the public.'

There may be no one better in racing than Dettori to help communicate the sport's position should the tide of public opinion reach a tipping point, but even he may not have enough charm to fix the industry's current crisis, stable staffing.

'Racing is time-consuming and hard work, a lot of people these days don't want to do it, so as you'll see in most of the stables, I'd say about 75 per cent are from a foreign country.

'I think people in this day and age want a nine-to-five job, they don't want to bust their ass and do all the extra hours when people from another country are willing to do it.

'Brexit could be an issue. They're not going to put a wall up like Donald Trump, but reading between the lines they will put a cap on it [immigration]. In my stable we have staff from six or seven different countries – we have Italian, Czech, Brazilian, Portuguese, Indian, Paki-

A touching moment as Ryan Moore and Frankie Dettori join hands after the Breeders' Cup Turf

stani, the whole shebang. That's the way racing has gone. When I came over, I was the foreigner – and I lived only two hours away!' Long since a certified Anglophile, Dettori has taken Britain to his heart in the same way racing the world over has taken him to its own. The sport needs a familiar, friendly public face now more than ever, and his willingness to serve as unofficial racing ambassador should not be taken for granted, for it is not an easy one – possibly an exhausting one.

The young jockey who once thought he could make a living out of riding has now conquered the racing world. Long may it continue, for there'll only ever be one Frankie.

Enable was the mare who kept on giving. Could it continue in the same vein in 2019?

RACING POST RATINGS VIEW – SAM WALKER

The Breeders' Cup Turf provided another opportunity for Enable to improve her sensational CV, but the form of the race gives another hint that she's not quite the same horse this year.

Taken in the context of her career this is not necessarily a bad thing – if she can become the first horse to win the Prix de l'Arc de Triomphe and follow up at the Breeders' Cup while below her best she's clearly quite something.

It is obvious that if you sit this year's form against what she did in 2017, when she won five Group 1s, including a King George and an Arc by margins of two and a half to five and a half lengths, she is clearly operating at a slightly lower level.

She posted a Racing Post Rating of 122 for her three-quarter-length success over Magical (121) in the Turf at Churchill Downs, which matches the figure she produced when winning the Arc by a short neck on her previous start.

To be fair it is often hard to produce a big rating around the tight tracks at the Breeders' Cup, and Enable's figure of 122 sits at the higher end of recent Turf winners.

She is 4-1 to land a third Arc next year and, assuming she races on, with an injury-free run she might be able to get closer to her three-year-old form, but I wouldn't bank on it and her recent level of form would make her vulnerable in a strong Arc.

8848a **LONGINES BREEDERS' CUP TURF (GRADE 1) (3YO+) (TURF)** **1m 4f (T)**
8:56 3-Y-O+
£1,629,629 (£503,703; £266,666; £148,148; £88,888; £2,962)

			RPR
1		**Enable**27 8026 4-8-11 0 ... FrankieDettori 2 (John Gosden) *in tch in midfield towards outer: tk clsr order 4f out: rdn to ld 2f out: pressed by runner-up fr under 2f out but kpt on strly and hld on wl: rdn out* **8/13**1	124+
2	¾	**Magical (IRE)**14 8406 3-8-7 0 ... RyanMoore 5 (A P O'Brien, Ire) *midfield: hdwy to trck ldrs 2 1/2f out: rdn 2f out: pressed wnr fr under 2f out: kpt on strly: a jst hld* **13/2**3	123
3	*9*	**Sadler's Joy (USA)**35 7794 5-9-0 0 ... JavierCastellano 11 (Thomas Albertrani, U.S.A) *hld up towards rr: gd hdwy on outer fr under 3f out: wd into st: rdn 2f out: wnt 3rd over 1f out: outpcd by front pair and hung lft ins fnl f: kpt on* **80/1**	110
4	*2*	**Arklow (USA)**16 4-9-0 0 ... FlorentGeroux 6 (Brad H Cox, U.S.A) *towards rr of midfield: rdn under 3f out: drvn and kpt on steadily fr over 1f out: hung lft ins fnl f* **100/1**	107
5	*1 ½*	**Waldgeist**27 8026 4-9-0 0 ... Pierre-CharlesBoudot 12 (A Fabre, France) *towards rr of midfield: rdn and effrt 2 1/2f out: wknd fnl f* **9/2**2	105
6	*4 ¼*	**Talismanic**27 8026 5-9-0 0 ... MickaelBarzalona 1 (A Fabre, France) *in tch on inner: nt clr run and lost pl 2 1/2f out: sn rdn and no imp* **16/1**	98
7	*½*	**Robert Bruce (CHI)**35 7794 4-9-0 0 ... IradOrtizJr 4 (Chad C Brown, U.S.A) *midfield: rdn 2 1/2f out: wknd fnl f* **16/1**	97
8	*¾*	**Hunting Horn (IRE)**27 8026 3-8-10 0 ... WayneLordan 13 (A P O'Brien, Ire) *in tch in midfield: tk clsr order on outer fr 5f out: prom 3 1/2f out: rdn 2 1/2f out: wknd 2f out: hmpd 1 1/2f out* **66/1**	97
9	*4 ½*	**Hi Happy (ARG)**26 6-9-0 0 ... LuisSaez 10 (Todd Pletcher, U.S.A) *trckd ldrs: led 4f out: rdn 2 1/2f out: hdd 2f out: sn wknd* **80/1**	89
10	*10 ¾*	**Quarteto De Cordas (BRZ)**91 4-9-0 0 ... BrianJosephHernandezJr 9 (Ian R Wilkes, U.S.A) *a towards rr* **100/1**	72
11	*8 ¾*	**Channel Maker (CAN)**35 7794 4-9-0 0 ... (b) JoseLOrtiz 3 (William Mott, U.S.A) *chsd ldr: lost pl 2 1/2f out: sn wl btn* **16/1**	58
12	*18 ½*	**Liam The Charmer (USA)**34 5-9-0 0 ... (b) TylerGaffalione 8 (Michael McCarthy, U.S.A) *a towards rr* **100/1**	
13	*3 ¼*	**Glorious Empire (IRE)**70 6568 7-9-0 ... JulienRLeparoux 7 (James Lawrence II, U.S.A) *led: hdd 4f out: lost pl 2 1/2f out. sn wl btn* **40/1**	

2m 32.65s
WFA 3 from 4yo+ 5lb **13** Ran SP% **120.5**
PARI-MUTUEL (all including 2 unit stake): WIN 3.60; PLACE (1-2) 3.00, 6.80; SHOW (1-2-3) 2.60, 4.80, 8.80; SF 26.80.
Owner K Abdullah **Bred** Juddmonte Farms Ltd **Trained** Newmarket, Suffolk

6
CORAL
ENABLE

NINE

CORAL-ECLIPSE STAKES

Sandown, July 6, 2019

Previous spread: Frankie Dettori is all smiles after Enable returns to the racecourse with victory in the Coral-Eclipse at Sandown in July 2019

3.35 RACE 4 *Coral-Eclipse (Group 1) (British Champions Series) (Class 1)* **ITV**
Winner £425,325 (1m 1f 209y) **1m2f**

£750,000 guaranteed **For** 3yo+ NOTE: Horses will only be eligible to run in this race provided that they have a current BHA Handicap Rating of 80 or higher at midday of the confirmation stage. Horses which do not qualify for a rating may also be eligible providing the BHA Handicapper is satisfied that the horse s racecourse performances up to and including the day before confirmation merit a provisional assessment of 80 or higher. Horses which have not run will not be eligible. **Weights** 3yo colts & geldings 8st 11lb; fillies 8st 8lb; 4yo+ colts & geldings 9st 7lb; fillies 9st 4lb **Weight for age** 3 from 4yo+ 10lb **Entries** 13 pay £3275 **1st Forfeit** 43 pay £3750 **Confirmed** 43 pay £2350.00 **Penalty value 1st** £425,325 **2nd** £161,250 **3rd** £80,700 **4th** £40,200 **5th** £20,175 **6th** £10,125

594-131 **1** (1) **DANCETERIA (FR)** 26 D4 S2 F2 C1 — 4 9-7
b g Redoute's Choice-Bal De La Rose — **Jamie Spencer**
David Menuisier Australian Bloodstock & Clive Washbourn — (119)

8-33444 **2** (3) **HUNTING HORN (IRE)** 17 D2 S1 F1 — 4 9-7
b c Camelot-Mora Bai — [1] **P B Beggy**
A P O'Brien (IRE) Mrs John Magnier & Michael Tabor & Derrick Smith — (123)

110-317 **3** (5) **MUSTASHRY** 18 F3 CD1 — 6 9-7
b/br g Tamayuz-Safwa — **Jim Crowley**
Sir Michael Stoute Hamdan Al Maktoum — (129)

6133-31 **4** (4) **REGAL REALITY** 44 S1 F2 CD1 — 4 9-7
b c Intello-Regal Realm — [1] **Kerrin McEvoy**
Sir Michael Stoute Cheveley Park Stud — ↑ (126)

102-117 **5** (2) **ZABEEL PRINCE (IRE)** 17 S4 F1 — 6 9-7
ch g Lope de Vega-Princess Serena — **Andrea Atzeni**
Roger Varian Sheikh Mohammed Obaid Al Maktoum — (127)

11/111- **6** (8) **ENABLE** 245 S3 F1 — 5 9-4
b m Nathaniel-Concentric — **Frankie Dettori**
John Gosden K Abdullah — (136)

12-1112 **7** (7) **MAGICAL (IRE)** 17 BF D2 S5 F2 — 4 9-4
b f Galileo-Halfway To Heaven — **Ryan Moore**
A P O'Brien (IRE) Derrick Smith & Mrs John Magnier & Michael Tabor — (133)

2110 **8** (6) **TELECASTER** 35 D2 F1 — 3 8-11
b c New Approach-Shirocco Star — **Oisin Murphy**
Hughie Morrison Castle Down Racing — (123)

2018 (7 ran) **Roaring Lion** (7) John Gosden 3 8-11 7/4F Oisin Murphy RPR123

BETTING FORECAST: 10-11 Enable, 3 Magical, 13-2 Regal Reality, 12 Telecaster, 14 Mustashry, 20 Zabeel Prince, 50 Danceteria, Hunting Horn.

JOHN GOSDEN WAS keen not to push Enable too much in the spring of 2019 with a third Arc in October the main target for the year.

By March she was back cantering, with the Coronation Cup at Epsom mooted as a possible return date. However, with the Epsom Group 1 being run earlier than normal connections then decided on Royal Ascot – either the Prince of Wales's Stakes or Hardwicke Stakes – as a starting point for Enable.

Her reappearance was pushed back further as Gosden felt that Royal Ascot would come soon and it was better for all concerned to aim her at the Coral-Eclipse.

Six days before the Sandown Group 1, Gosden said: 'It's her first run back and you know the main target is on the first Sunday

Enable and Frankie Dettori are led to the Al Bahathri gallop in Newmarket by groom Imran Shahwani in June 2019

in October. We'll try to build to that but we're happy with her. She's showing her enjoyment in training and her eagerness. Her exuberant nature is back and she has slimmed down a bit. I couldn't be more happy with her work.'

Jockey Robert Havlin was a key player for Gosden when it came to readying horses for the big day. He discussed the finishing touches to Enable's preparations:

We're all looking forward to seeing Enable back in action in the Coral-Eclipse and this is absolutely the right race to be starting her back in.

Up until the last two or three weeks she was telling us she wasn't ready to run. The boss always does what's best for his horses and one of his greatest strengths is knowing when a horse is ready and not asking them to do too much before then.

I've only ridden her a few times this year, which is the same situation for Frankie, so it's her lad Imran Shahwani who has done a lot of the work with her.

Enable and Frankie Dettori work behind her lead horse on the Al Bahathri gallop

I rode Enable in her last piece of work for the Eclipse on Wednesday, Frankie rode her on the Saturday before that and the Wednesday, so he's had a good chance to sit on her to get ready for this race.

It really wasn't until she switched on to the grass that we saw the real Enable. She was working along on the Al Bahathri but not really doing what she can.

However, as soon as she came on to the grass she really came alive; she loves the grass and that was the first time I got to ride her this season. She was brilliant.

I've ridden Enable in three bits of work this year which have all been in the last few weeks and she's been nothing but amazing for me.

It's just been a case of waiting for the right time, and that's exactly what the boss has been doing. I'd say it's his biggest asset as a trainer, the same as Sir Michael Stoute. He never rushes his horses and he gives them the time to come to themselves and to come to their best.

Enable is telling us that now is the time.

It was indeed time as Lee Mottershead reported from Sandown:

The world's most famous jockey, the world's most famous racehorse and the greatest union of man and beast racing has to offer got the pulse of Sandown beating fast and hard as Enable and Frankie Dettori reminded us once more that theirs is a marriage of magnificence.

A racecourse that normally saves rapturous receptions for jumping's winter heroes came alive on a sunny summer afternoon graced by a wondermare who returned from a 245-day absence to stamp her name on the Coral-Eclipse roll of honour.

In itself it was a marvellous achievement but it promised so much more, for the raison d'etre behind Enable staying in training at five has been the pursuit of a holy grail. No horse has ever won three Prix de l'Arc de Triomphes. That glorious goal now seems ever more attainable.

After a three-quarter-length defeat of old rival Magical that was more authoritative than the margin suggested, Dettori declared Enable the best horse he has ridden. As a 48-year-old colossus of the sport he has ridden quite a few and, 16 days on from his unforgettable Royal Ascot four-timer, he rode three more winners, each

Enable follows Magical down the horsewalk at Sandown before the Coral-Eclipse

one greeted by enormous ovations. The people adore him. When he rides Enable they adore him even more.

In turn, his affection for Khalid Abdullah's incredible lady is obvious. After passing the winning post he punched the air before stroking Enable's left ear. Then he soaked up the sounds.

'I can't even hear myself talk at the moment, it's amazing,' he said. 'She's special and this touches me. I love her so much.'

John Gosden no doubt feels the same. He loves her and he knows her, which is why he was content to be patient, bypassing first the Coronation Cup and then the Prince of Wales's Stakes. From one morning to the next he waited to see signs the now eight-time Group 1 winner was ready to dazzle.

It was worth the wait. Enable's sire Nathaniel won the Eclipse first time out and now so has his daughter. Running over a mile and a quarter for only the second time – her only career defeat had come at the trip – she sat second behind Hunting Horn before leading over two furlongs from home. From there to the line the result was never truly in doubt.

Enable stays on strongly to beat old rival Magical by three-quarters of a length in the Coral-Eclipse

'As we turned for home she grabbed the bit and she wanted to go,' said Dettori. 'I was saying to her: "Let's just wait a little bit – let's get to the two-pole first!" She then quickened and put the race to bed. We were very confident but knew the race would bring her on. What a great filly!

'She has so many gears and an unbelievable will to win. She has everything – the size, the scope and the stride. She can go on any ground and over any distance.'

Is she, therefore, at the top of his personal all-time list? 'I would say so, yes,' said Dettori. 'She has the best CV of any horse I've ridden. You could argue Golden Horn was better but Enable's longevity has been incredible. Let's enjoy her while we've got her.'

One could say the same about the evergreen Italian, who after performing a flying dismount was acclaimed with cheers of, 'Oh, Frankie Dettori', belted out to the Seven Nation Army tune that greeted Jeremy Corbyn at Glastonbury two years ago. As they sang, Kerrin McEvoy watched from the weighing-room steps, having turned around to see Enable and her jockey afforded the respect

John Gosden looks on as Enable and Frankie Dettori take in the applause in the Sandown winner's enclosure

they deserve. McEvoy smiled. When he goes home there will be a story to tell.

Gosden told a good one when detailing what happened in the weeks leading up to Enable – who he assessed here as no more than 90 per cent fit – joining Pebbles and Kooyonga as an Eclipse heroine.

'It's great to have her back,' he said. 'She's very competitive but that didn't really begin to show until the last 14 days, at which point suddenly the edge came back. It was very apparent in the way she was carrying herself and her behaviour. If you now go in her box you know it's her space and if you mess around in there she'll split you in two.

'Before that she was doing everything perfectly but the hunger wasn't there. She was just going through the motions. She wasn't concentrating but then she became fitter, quicker and sharper, just like a boxer. She suddenly went into the zone.

'Any of the professional tennis players will tell you that you have to get back into that zone. She came back into it over the last two weeks. You need to have incredible mental strength, like tennis

Opposite page: Enable and Frankie Dettori land the Coral-Eclipse at Sandown

KPP

players when it's six-all in the fifth set. The great athletes and the great horses have it – and she has it."

She has it and we will next see her using it at Ascot when she seeks to regain the King George VI and Queen Elizabeth Stakes.

After that it will be York – Gosden prefers the Yorkshire Oaks to the Juddmonte International – and then the Arc, in which she will attempt to do what even Treve could not do four years ago. Should she make it to Paris on October's first Sunday, she will be the one being cheered loudest, just as Abdullah's racing manager Teddy Grimthorpe observed young tennis sensation Coco Gauff was cheered loudest ten miles away at Wimbledon.

'She is very loveable,' said Grimthorpe of Enable. 'I think the sporting public take to humans like Coco and horses like Enable. They love these girls who put it all on the line and come good. She's now getting into people's psyche. It all adds up to a great story.'

Now, following this happy day, we move closer to what should be one of the very greatest stories.

'The Arc is always in the back of our minds,' added Grimthorpe. 'The whole reason for keeping her in training is to try to make history. She has taken the first step towards making it.'

Ten years after winning the Eclipse on Sea The Stars, former top jockey Mick Kinane was quick to pay tribute to Dettori:

Frankie Dettori is riding like a man possessed and Mick Kinane knows exactly why.

Ten years ago Kinane had just turned 50 and won the Eclipse for the fourth time, aboard the exceptional Sea The Stars. He found that one horse transformed his confidence and recognises a similar story with the bubbling Dettori.

Dettori, 48, topped the table at Royal Ascot for the first time in 15 years last month.

Here Enable gave him his second of three winners on the day, a sixth Group 1 win since the start of the season and a sixth of seven wins from his last 11 rides. Dettori is not just hot, he is molten.

At the moment it seems whenever he looms into a race there is almost an inevitability about the outcome. The crowds at Ascot and Sandown certainly felt it. So did Kinane.

Frankie Dettori is greeted by John Gosden after his Coral-Eclipse victory on Enable

The 60-year-old legend of the saddle said: 'You see the reaction today – even when the stalls opened there was a big cheer from the crowd and you don't hear that often in Flat racing. The reception coming in was great. He's one very talented jockey; great for the game.'

But for Kinane it was not just a brilliant performance from a wonderful horse, watching Dettori prompted humour and reflection. Enable has come along at a very similar point in Dettori's career as Sea The Stars did in his, and watching on took him back.

Asked why Dettori is riding so well, the Irish wit flashed. 'He doesn't have me to hassle him anymore,' he said with a laugh. But the question was given ample consideration. 'That's what good horses do for you, they put a spring in your step. That's what Sea The Stars did for me when he arrived late in my career. It gives you a new lease of life – it's like a transfusion.'

It is not just Dettori who Kinane is full of admiration for. Enable, like Sea The Stars, has only been defeated once, very early in her career. She rattled off a sequence as a three-year-old, winning five Group 1s in four months, and has since added three more. This autumn she will attempt to match Kinane's total of three Arc victories – something no horse has ever done.

Kinane said: 'She's one of the all-time greats, and if she can go on and win a third Arc it'd be something else.'

Trainer Aidan O'Brien was also quick to praise Enable after Magical had re-enacted their showdown in the Breeders' Cup Turf over two furlongs further eight months earlier.

'It's a privilege to be here and see her,' said O'Brien. 'She's a great filly, we all know that.'

Connections then revealed that the King George VI and Queen Elizabeth Stakes would be Enable's next target in her quest for a third Prix de l'Arc de Triomphe.

RACING POST RATINGS VIEW – **PAUL CURTIS**

While not needing to match her very best form, Enable left the strong impression that she's as good as ever in winning the Coral-Eclipse, producing a Racing Post Rating of 124+ despite conceding race fitness to her rivals over a trip short of her best.

She also didn't quite replicate her three-year-old form (129) or last year's three victories, but that's not to say she can't. Even on this form she'll take all the beating over a mile and a half, and although this form ties her in closely with Prince of Wales's victor Crystal Ocean through Magical, she'll surely improve for the run.

The Eclipse form itself looks sound, with Magical (122) giving her pacemaker Hunting Horn a similar beating to Ascot, and the improving Regal Reality finding further progress to an RPR of 121 in backing up his previous course-and-distance defeat of subsequent winner Matterhorn.

4668 **CORAL-ECLIPSE (GROUP 1) (BRITISH CHAMPIONS SERIES)** **1m 1f 209y**
3:35 (3:40) (Class 1) 3-Y-O+

£425,325 (£161,250; £80,700; £40,200; £20,175; £10,125) **Stalls** Low

Form				RPR
111-	**1**		**Enable**[245] 8848 5-9-4 125 .... FrankieDettori 8 (John Gosden) *trckd ldr: led over 2f out: shkn up over 1f out: styd on strly and nvr in serious danger fnl f* **4/6**[1]	124+
1112	**2**	*¾*	**Magical (IRE)**[17] 3985 4-9-4 123 .... RyanMoore 7 (A P O'Brien, Ire) *trckd ldng pair: shkn up over 2f out: rdn to chse wnr wl over 1f out: styd on wl but nvr able to seriously threaten* **11/4**[2]	122
3-31	**3**	*2*	**Regal Reality**[44] 3025 4-9-7 116 .... KerrinMcEvoy 4 (Sir Michael Stoute) *fractious on to crse and taken whole lap of trck to post: dwlt: hld up in last trio: prog over 2f out: rdn to chse ldng pair over 1f out: styd on same pce after* **17/2**[3]	121
-131	**4**	*2½*	**Danceteria (FR)**[26] 3678 4-9-7 110 .... JamieSpencer 1 (David Menuisier) *hld up and sn in last: rdn and detached over 2f out: styd on fnl f to take 4th last strides* **50/1**	116
-310	**5**	*hd*	**Mustashry**[18] 3948 6-9-7 121 .... JimCrowley 5 (Sir Michael Stoute) *hld up in last trio: gng strly 3f out: rdn and nt qckn 2f out: one pce after* **12/1**	116
3444	**6**	*nk*	**Hunting Horn (IRE)**[17] 3985 4-9-7 114 .... PBBeggy 3 (A P O'Brien, Ire) *led at str pce: stdd 1/2-way: rdn and hdd over 2f out: steadily wknd* **33/1**	115
2110	**7**	*2¼*	**Telecaster**[35] 3345 3-8-11 115 .... OisinMurphy 6 (Hughie Morrison) *failed to parade: trckd ldrs in 5th shkn up over 2f out: no rspnse and dropped to last fnl f* **10/1**	111
-110	**8**	*nk*	**Zabeel Prince (IRE)**[17] 3985 6-9-7 117 .... AndreaAtzeni 2 (Roger Varian) *trckd ldng trio: rdn over 2f out: wknd over 1f out* **20/1**	109

2m 4.77s (-5.43) **Going Correction** -0.125s/f (Firm)
WFA 3 from 4yo+ 10lb **8** Ran SP% **123.6**
Speed ratings (Par 117): **116,115,113,111,111 111,109,109**
CSF £3.01 CT £9.14 TOTE £1.50: £1.10, £1.20, £2.50; EX 3.10 Trifecta £10.50.
Owner K Abdullah **Bred** Juddmonte Farms Ltd **Trained** Newmarket, Suffolk

TEN

KING GEORGE VI AND QUEEN ELIZABETH STAKES

July 27, 2019

Previous spread: Enable claims a pulsating triumph over Crystal Ocean in the King George VI and Queen Elizabeth Stakes at Ascot in July 2019

3.40 RACE 4

King George VI And Queen Elizabeth Qipco Stakes (Group 1) (British Champions Series) (Class 1) **ITV**

Winner £708,875 (1m 3f 211y) **1m4f**

£1,250,000 guaranteed **For** 3yo+ NOTE: Horses will only be eligible to run in this race provided that they have a current BHA Handicap Rating of 80 or higher at midday of the confirmation stage. Horses which do not qualify for a rating may also be eligible providing the BHA Handicapper is satisfied that the horse's racecourse performances up to and including the day before confirmation merit a provisional assessment of 80 or higher. Horses which have not run will not be eligible. **Weights** 3yo colts & geldings 8st 10lb; fillies 8st 7lb; 4yo+ colts & geldings 9st 7lb; fillies 9st 4lb **Weight for age** 3 from 4yo+ 11lb **pay £5450 1st Forfeit** 18 pay £6250 **2nd Forfeit** 11 pay £3925 **Confirmed** 11 **Penalty value 1st** £708,875 **2nd** £268,750 **3rd** £134,500 **4th** £67,000 **5th** £33,625 **6th** £16,875

Form / No. (Draw)	Horse / Breeding / Trainer, Owner	Age Wt / Jockey / RPR
02443-2 **1** (6)	**CHEVAL GRAND** (JPN) 119 D4 F6 *ch h Heart's Cry-Halwa Sweet* **Yasuo Tomomichi (JPN)** Kazuhiro Sasaki	7 9-7 [1]**Oisin Murphy** 127
222-111 **2** (9)	**CRYSTAL OCEAN** 38 D3 S3 F4 C1 CD1 *b h Sea The Stars-Crystal Star* **Sir Michael Stoute** Sir Evelyn De Rothschild	5 9-7 [1]**James Doyle** 135
02-4211 **3** (3)	**DEFOE** (IRE) 35 D3 S4 CD1 *gr g Dalakhani-Dulkashe* **Roger Varian** Sheikh Mohammed Obaid Al Maktoum	5 9-7 **Andrea Atzeni** 129
-334446 **4** (10)	**HUNTING HORN** (IRE) 21 S1 F1 C1 *b c Camelot-Mora Bai* **A P O'Brien (IRE)** Mrs John Magnier & Michael Tabor & Derrick Smith	p1 4 9-7 **Seamie Heffernan** 123
521-184 **5** (2)	**MORANDO** (FR) 35 D1 S4 *gr g Kendargent-Moranda* **Andrew Balding** King Power Racing Co Ltd	6 9-7 [1]**P J McDonald** 127
369-137 **6** (5)	**SALOUEN** (IRE) 35 S1 F2 CD1 *b h Canford Cliffs-Gali Gal* **Sylvester Kirk** H Balasuriya	5 9-7 [1]**Jim Crowley** 125
1455-13 **7** (4)	**WALDGEIST** 38 D4 S4 *ch h Galileo-Waldlerche* **A Fabre (FR)** Gestut Ammerland & Newsells Park	5 9-7 **Pierre-Charles Boudot** 130
1/111-1 **8** (11)	**ENABLE** 21 D7 S3 F2 CD1 *b m Nathaniel-Concentric* **John Gosden** K Abdullah	5 9-4 **Frankie Dettori** 136
4-25322 **9** (1)	**MAGIC WAND** (IRE) 29 F1 CD1 *b f Galileo-Prudenzia* **A P O'Brien (IRE)** Michael Tabor & Derrick Smith & Mrs John Magnier	p1 4 9-4 **Donnacha O'Brien** 124
239-112 **10** (7)	**ANTHONY VAN DYCK** (IRE) 28 BF D2 S2 F2 *b c Galileo-Believe'n'succeed* **A P O'Brien (IRE)** Mrs John Magnier & Michael Tabor & Derrick Smith	p1 3 8-10 **Ryan Moore** 126
14-2893 **11** (8)	**NORWAY** (IRE) 28 F1 *ch c Galileo-Love Me True* **A P O'Brien (IRE)** Derrick Smith & Mrs John Magnier & Michael Tabor	p 3 8-10 [1]**Wayne Lordan** 115

2018 (7 ran) **Poet's Word** (8) Sir Michael Stoute 5 9-7 7/4 James Doyle RPR128

BETTING FORECAST: 8-13 Enable, 11-4 Crystal Ocean, 8 Anthony Van Dyck, 14 Defoe, Waldgeist, 33 Cheval Grand, 50 Magic Wand, 66 Morando, Salouen, 100 Hunting Horn, Norway.

IT WAS NOW all systems go for the King George VI and Queen Elizabeth Stakes, a race John Gosden billed as a British version of the Arc after Enable cantered in front of the media ten days before Ascot's midsummer showpiece.

He said: 'The battle of the generations is what the King George is all about – it's like a British version of the Arc.

'There was a time when it had become a four-year-old only race but not this year.'

Enable, who her trainer said was 'highly unlikely' to remain in training at six, started her campaign later than planned at Sandown after failing to show her customary sparkle at home in late spring.

He added: 'We missed Epsom and Ascot, and it was only when she got on the Limekilns round gallop before Sandown that she showed her old zest. Before that she was like an old heavyweight doing the roads and going in the gym and going through the motions.'

On the special qualities of the daughter of Nathaniel, Gosden added: 'What makes Enable so special is that she's got great physique, great depth and has a wonderful mind on her. Frankie says when she stretches in the latter part of a race he can actually feel his legs move.

'Another great attribute is that she has a lot of tactical speed as she showed at Sandown and is effective at a mile and a quarter to a mile and a half.'

Enable had to battle hard to deny Crystal Ocean in a race for the ages at Ascot. Peter Scargill reported:

John Gosden's eyes said it all. After one of the greatest and most pulsating races ever seen, one in which the magnificent champion Enable was forced to dig into her very core to find what was needed to defeat Crystal Ocean, the champion trainer was wide-eyed with adrenaline and awe.

Gosden does not normally look like that after races but what he – and the millions watching around the world – had witnessed was not a normal race, not even close.

A relaxed Enable is led across Ascot High Street by groom Imran Shahwani before the King George

It was an epic. A battle between two brilliant horses and jockeys that evoked memories of some of the finest races ever run. Perhaps it even was the finest race ever run.

'You had the best older horse and the best older filly taking on horses with that level of quality and they outclassed the whole field,' Gosden said. 'It was a proper King George – what more could racing have asked for? Crystal Ocean said to her "I'm going to win this" and she said back "no, I am", and she really showed mental toughness and so did he. She showed a lot of guts.'

Having been drawn widest of all in stall 11, Enable was held wide by her opponents as a blistering pace was set, forcing Frankie Dettori to take her back twice to find a comfortable position towards the rear.

Dettori forfeited ground to his rivals, but turning for home he knew Crystal Ocean was the only horse he needed to beat. With a quarter of a mile to run, Frankie said 'go'.

The champion mare engaged the overdrive that had taken her to glory in two Arcs, three Oaks, a Coral-Eclipse and a Breeders' Cup

Enable is led around the pre-parade ring at Ascot

but Crystal Ocean, the embodiment of tenacity and determination, would not lie down.

He fought for all his worth, he edged his head back in front of the wondermare and he called on all he had as the two warriors pulled away from their rivals. Yet Enable, the supreme being that she is, would not wilt either and the victory was hers as unbridled joy erupted among the energised and appreciative crowd.

Dettori, so often frenetic in victory, was physically and emotionally drained by the experience, although his legions of fans were still treated to an enthusiastic flying dismount.

'I don't want too many races like that because I'm absolutely exhausted,' he said. 'In all my career that was the hardest fought big race I've had, with two champions fighting it out.

'Give credit to Crystal Ocean, he put it out there for me and it was an amazing race. He was a bit like one of those flies that wouldn't go away and he was always there annoying me to the line.

'I knew he was the one to beat as he's very strong around here and once I put my head in front I thought I was going to see it out. In

2
QIPCO
CRYSTAL OCEAN

Previous spread: Enable wins the King George by a neck from Crystal Ocean at Ascot

Right: John Gosden savours the moment after Enable wins the King George for the second time

fairness he served it up to me and we had a right titanic battle, but I always had the edge.'

Gosden felt Enable's neck margin of victory was possibly reduced by having to go earlier than planned, and said: 'I said to Frankie before the race to stay cool and he did. I thought he hit the front too soon and I kept saying to myself, "no, no wait", although I'm sure the great jockey will tell me why he moved then.'

Enable was pushed out to 7-4 favourite (from 6-4) by Betfair for her attempt at an historic third win in the Qatar Prix de l'Arc de Triomphe at Longchamp in October, and with her final stage drawing ever closer Dettori was eager to saviour the moment.

'She's extraordinary and she even surprised me today,' he said. 'She's an amazing horse in every way: her ability, her courage, how uncomplicated she is. I don't know what to say, I love her.

'She gives me emotions that no other horse has ever given to me in my life and she's only with me for another three months, so I'm trying to capture and enjoy every moment as we're probably only going to see her two more times. Let's enjoy her because she's a superstar.'

York, for the Yorkshire Oaks or the Juddmonte International, and Paris had been connections' plan for Enable, although whether she races again in Britain will depend on the after-effects of Ascot and the potential impact of another race on her Arc challenge.

Teddy Grimthorpe, racing manager for owner-breeder Khalid Adbullah, said: 'What more can you say about her? That was a race for the ages.

'I think we've given up pre-guessing her. Last time we thought she'd had a hard race she was bucking and kicking the next day and had eaten up and everything. The main target is the Arc and if we thought it was best not to go to York then that's fine – we need to do what's best for her.'

If this is the final time we see Enable on these shores then what a memory she, and Crystal Ocean, have left us. Our eyes will be blessed to ever see something as spectacular again.

Graham Dench analysed the King George from a tactical point of view:

John Gosden and Frankie Dettori were obviously alive to the likelihood of the King George becoming tactical, with four Ballydoyle horses in opposition, and they will also have been alive to the possibility of unexpected tactics being employed.

Enable lands the King George after a thrilling battle with Crystal Ocean up the home straight at Ascot

As we all did, they also knew that despite the Aidan O'Brien's quartet being headed by a Derby winner, the one to beat on all known form was Crystal Ocean.

Most expected Hunting Horn, who was drawn immediately to Enable's inner – the pair occupying the two widest stalls – to go on and help force the pace, but instead he was initially held back, which kept her wide, while Norway forced a furious gallop.

Dettori was therefore obliged to take a pull and drop her in behind him, and also behind Crystal Ocean, further back than intended.

The pace set by Norway, who raced clear of Magic Wand and Hunting Horn, ought to have suited Anthony Van Dyck, who was perfectly placed on the inner, but it was clear four out he was not going to be a factor and when Norway drifted off the rail turning in only Hunting Horn was close enough to take advantage.

Enable meanwhile had made her move on the outer, picking off her rivals one by one and getting there so quickly she straightened up on Crystal Ocean's quarters, with Norway only just in front.

From two out it was a straight match and for a moment Enable looked as though she might come clear, but she had done plenty of running to get there and Crystal Ocean is a formidable opponent.

Hard though he fought, Enable always just had the upper hand and Dettori gave her just one smack, around a furlong and a half out, and then waved the whip in front of her left eye before putting it down, merely pushing her out through the last 100 yards.

It was an epic finish to an epic race, but there was only going to be one winner.

Lee Mottershead reflected on a unforgettable afternoon:

It may not have been her best performance, and on the figures she will not even be recorded as the best horse, but Enable has yet to bless us with a memory finer than that she created on one of British Flat racing's most unforgettable afternoons.

When two horses fight out a furious finish at Ascot, and most especially when that happens in the track's most important prize, comparisons are made with what took place in 1975 when Grundy and Bustino were responsible for what was christened race of the century. There are some who see it as sacrilege to place anything else on the same pedestal, but to say this day had echoes of that day is not fanciful.

A physically and emotionally drained Frankie Dettori after Enable's mesmerising King George victory

For Crystal Ocean there were further echoes, in his case of last year's King George VI and Queen Elizabeth Stakes. Now, as then, he gave his everything. His everything was not enough. He is a magnificent animal, the epitome of a competitor, and in defeat he lost nothing except first place. His latest misfortune was that the rival eyeballing him throughout the final two furlongs is an athlete who has become addicted to winning.

To win this race she had to do it hard and tough, just as Grundy had in 1975. In Bustino's corner were two pacemakers, Highest and Kinglet, who went like the clappers in a fruitless bid to squeeze every last drop of energy out of Grundy. Anthony Van Dyck was not Enable'smain threat but the Derby winner had three stablemates to support him and they raced one, two and three, Norway leading the way at a scorching gallop. But there was more to it than that.

Hunting Horn carried out the front-runner role in the Eclipse but on this occasion sat only third, one spot behind Magic Wand. Crucially, he began from stall ten, with only Enable wider on the track. With Seamie Heffernan showing some restraint, as he was perfectly entitled to do, Frankie Dettori was kept deep on the track through

Frankie Dettori performs a flying dismount from Enable in the Ascot winner's enclosure

the first furlong. He had to make a choice. Stay there or take a pull and drop back, mindful that might leave him with more ground to make up than he might ideally have wanted. He took the latter decision.

Aidan O'Brien loves to run pacemakers because he believes, with justification, they help to ensure the cream rises to the top. That was borne out once again, but with Anthony Van Dyck completely failing to fire, the cream came in the shape of Enable and Crystal Ocean.

Up Ascot's home straight they duelled, just as Grundy and Bustino had duelled 44 years earlier. When Enable took over from Crystal Ocean at the two pole – Enable always seems to lead at the two pole – she looked set to go clear, only for Crystal Ocean to rally with the utmost gameness. He drained all his reserves under James Doyle, but Enable, hit just once with Dettori's whip, was always doing fractionally enough.

Enable's entire season is built around her bid to make history by landing a third Prix de l'Arc de Triomphe. It is the reason she has been kept in training. However, Khalid Abdullah's bold decision has already been vindicated, for Enable is now one of only three horses to win two King Georges. She has never lost when ridden by Dettori but when they join in union it is she who is the star, as he would be first to admit. That is the measure of the horse.

While Abdullah's racing manager Teddy Grimthorpe was talking to the press he caught sight of Dettori. 'You'll have to excuse me,' he said. 'I'm going for a cuddle.' He duly went for his cuddle, but the man on the other end of the embrace soon seemed almost emotionally exhausted, his state not helped by a cold.

'The gloves were off and she really surprised me,' he said. 'I don't think we've ever seen a more competitive finish. You probably have to go back to Grundy-Bustino.'

Go back that far and there is the uncomfortable reminder of the effect that encounter took on its two combatants. Bustino never ran again, while Grundy flopped at York on his only subsequent outing. Perhaps the difference between the winners of these two epic King Georges is Grundy, although a dual Derby victor, is best remembered for his Ascot triumph. Enable has achieved much more and for much longer. She is a bigger deal.

That is not to denigrate him but to hail her – and also Crystal Ocean, from whom she was receiving the 3lb sex allowance. John Gosden's handling of Enable has been exquisite, but so, too, has the way in which Stoute brought his brave servant to this point. He knew the enormity of what he had seen and uncharacteristically hung around by the weighing room for some time after it was all over. The reason for his wait became clear when Dettori, his media commitments completed, finally made it back to the weighing room, where the trainer he had so narrowly denied put an arm on the successful jockey's shoulder. It was a nice touch.

Frankie Dettori was Enable's chief cheerleader at Ascot

By then Enable was long gone, as was her groom Imran Shahwani. 'I shut my eyes,' he said. 'I know she never wants to give up but I couldn't watch her. I was shouting her name, and 95 per cent of me knew she was going to win, but it was still a race.'

Wasn't it just. It was one we shall remember forever, just as those who were at Ascot for the King George of 1975 still cherish the memories made that sunny afternoon.

Independently, Dettori and Doyle used the same phrase when recounting the exhilarating experience they had shared. 'What a race,' they both said.

What a race indeed. What a race!

Ascot witnessed one of the finest races in its long and illustrious history. It left Enable firmly on course for the Arc.

RACING POST RATINGS VIEW – **PAUL CURTIS**

Enable produced her best figure since her three-year-old days to hold the challenge of Crystal Ocean in an epic King George, returning a Racing Post Rating of 127+ that, given the unfavourable journey she endured, suggests she is at least as good as ever.

This form rates of very similar merit to her 2017 win in the race as a three-year-old when attaining an RPR of 128 and rates right up there with the best performances seen in the race this century.

She is clearly the best filly or mare in training, and with the sex allowance she sets a daunting target for the colts to aim at and a third Arc looks very much on the cards.

Crystal Ocean emerges with great credit and proved himself better than ever in going down narrowly, returning an RPR of 129. Bar Enable's 2017 win, such a level of performance would have been enough to secure the King George every year since Harbinger's 2010 romp and the five-year-old retains his position as the highest-rated horse in the world this year.

Waldgeist finished a lot closer to Crystal Ocean than when a never-nearer third in the Prince of Wales's Stakes and confirmed the impression from his winning reappearance in the Prix Ganay that he too had improved from four to five. Despite finishing a little further behind Enable than in last year's Arc, both horses ran better in a more truly run race and, in finishing seven lengths clear of the rest, Waldgeist looks well worth an RPR of 126.

This is the first time since Galileo beat Fantastic Light in 2001 that the first three in a King George have all been rated above 125, a testament to the quality of a top-class race.

5414 **KING GEORGE VI AND QUEEN ELIZABETH QIPCO STKS (GROUP 1) (BRITISH CHAMPIONS SERIES)** **1m 3f 211y**
3:40 (3:40) (Class 1) 3-Y-O+

£708,875 (£268,750; £134,500; £67,000; £33,625; £16,875) **Stalls** Low

Form RPR

11-1 **1** **Enable**[21] 4668 5-9-4 125 .... FrankieDettori 11 127
(John Gosden) *trapped out wd 1st 4f: hld up in last quartet: prog over 4f out: clsd qckly fr 3f out to ld 2f out: shkn up and pressed by runner-up after: narrow but decisive ld last 100yds and mostly pushed out nr fin* **8/15**[1]

-111 **2** *nk* **Crystal Ocean**[38] 3985 5-9-7 127 .... JamesDoyle 9 129
(Sir Michael Stoute) *trckd clr ldrs: prog to go 2nd 3f out: led over 2f out but sn pounced on by wnr and narrowly hdd: fought on bravely and stl upsides ins fnl f: narrowly but clrly hld last 100yds* **7/2**[2]

5-13 **3** *1 ¾* **Waldgeist**[38] 3985 5-9-7 122 .... Pierre-CharlesBoudot 4 126
(A Fabre, France) *hld up in midfield: hdwy over 3f out: 5th over 2f out: sn prog u.p to chse ldng pair: nvr able to chal and but styd on wl and edgd clsr nr fin* **12/1**

-130 **4** *7* **Salouen (IRE)**[35] 4093 5-9-7 115 .... JimCrowley 5 115
(Sylvester Kirk) *stdd s: hld up in last pair: sme prog 4f out: rdn 3f out: kpt on u.p fnl 2f to take modest 4th last strides* **80/1**

4446 **5** *nk* **Hunting Horn (IRE)**[21] 4668 4-9-7 115 .... (p[1]) SeamieHeffernan 10 114
(A P O'Brien, Ire) *prog to chse ldng pair after 2f: rdn to dispute 2nd briefly 3f out: wknd over 2f out: lost modest 4th last strides* **66/1**

/4-2 **6** *3 ½* **Cheval Grand (JPN)**[119] 1446 7-9-7 119 .... OisinMurphy 6 109
(Yasuo Tomomichi, Japan) *hld up in last quartet: sme prog over 3f out but u.p: nvr a threat but plugged on fnl 2f* **33/1**

2003 **7** *7* **Norway (IRE)**[28] 4414 3-8-10 104 .... (p) WayneLordan 8 99
(A P O'Brien, Ire) *led at blistering pce: hdd & wknd qckly over 2f out* **66/1**

-104 **8** *14* **Morando (FR)**[35] 4093 6-9-7 115 .... PJMcDonald 2 75
(Andrew Balding) *a in rr: toiling in last pl sn after 1/2-way: t.o* **66/1**

4211 **9** *nk* **Defoe (IRE)**[35] 4093 5-9-7 119 .... AndreaAtzeni 3 75
(Roger Varian) *a in rr: nt gng wl fr 5f out: wknd over 3f out: t.o* **10/1**

-112 **10** *5* **Anthony Van Dyck (IRE)**[28] 4414 3-8-10 118 .... (p[1]) RyanMoore 7 68
(A P O'Brien, Ire) *chsd ldng trio: rdn 5f out: wknd 4f out: t.o* **7/1**[3]

5322 **11** *11* **Magic Wand (IRE)**[29] 4354 4-9-4 109 .... (p[1]) DonnachaO'Brien 1 46
(A P O'Brien, Ire) *chsd ldr at str pce to 3f out: wknd rapidly: t.o* **28/1**

2m 32.42s (-0.18) **Going Correction** +0.55s/f (Yiel)
WFA 3 from 4yo+ 11lb **11** Ran SP% **128.8**
Speed ratings (Par 117): **122,121,120,115,115 113,108,99,99,95 88**
CSF £3.04 CT £14.23 TOTE £1.40: £1.10, £1.40, £3.10; EX 3.30 Trifecta £16.00.
Owner K Abdullah **Bred** Juddmonte Farms Ltd **Trained** Newmarket, Suffolk

sky bet
sky bet
sky bet
sky
1
Darley

ELEVEN

YORKSHIRE OAKS

York, August 22, 2019

Previous spread: Enable records a two-and-three-quarter-length victory over Magical to claim a second Yorkshire Oaks at York in August 2019

3.35 RACE 4 — *Darley Yorkshire Oaks (Group 1) (British Champions Series) (Fillies & Mares) (Class 1)* **ITV**

Winner £241,017.50 (1m 3f 188y) **1m4f**

£425,000 guaranteed **For** 3yo+ fillies and mares NOTE: Horses will only be eligible to run in this race provided that they have a current BHA Handicap Rating of 80 or higher at midday of the confirmation stage. Horses which do not qualify for a rating may also be eligible providing the BHA handicapper is satisfied the horse's racecourse performances up to and including the day before confirmation merit a a provisional assessment of 80 or higher. Horses which have not run will not be eligible **Weights** 3yo 8st 12lb; 4yo+ 9st 7lb **Weight for age** 3 from 4yo+ 9lb **pay £1750 1st Forfeit** 18 pay £2000 **2nd Forfeit** 1 pay £30000 **Confirmed** 7 pay £1250.00 **Penalty value 1st** £241,017.50 **2nd** £91,375 **3rd** £45,730 **4th** £22,780

/111-11 **ENABLE** 26 **D8 S4 F2 CD1** 5 9-7
1 *b m Nathaniel-Concentric* **Frankie Dettori** 134
(1) **John Gosden** K Abdullah

123-163 **LAH TI DAR** 53 **S1 F3 C1 CD1** 4 9-7
2 *b f Dubawi-Dar Re Mi* [1]**William Buick** 124
(2) **John Gosden** Lord Lloyd-Webber

2-11122 **MAGICAL (IRE)** 47 **D1 S5 F2** 4 9-7
3 *b f Galileo-Halfway To Heaven* **Ryan Moore** 130
(4) **A P O'Brien (IRE)** Derrick Smith & Mrs John Magnier & Michael Tabor

6314138 **SOUTH SEA PEARL (IRE)** 4 **D1** 3 8-12
4 *b f Galileo-Cassydora* **Seamie Heffernan** 111
(3) **A P O'Brien (IRE)** Derrick Smith & Mrs John Magnier & Michael Tabor

2018 (8 ran) **Sea Of Class** (5) William Haggas 3 8-12 7/4F James Doyle RPR120

BETTING FORECAST: 2-7 Enable, 7-2 Magical, 14 Lah Ti Dar, 50 South Sea Pearl.

AS THE DUST settled on a ninth Group 1 triumph it was revealed that Enable would run next in the Yorkshire Oaks.

Teddy Grimthorpe said: 'Having talked to Prince Khalid and John Gosden the plan is to go to the Darley Yorkshire Oaks. She won that race on her way to her first Arc, so there's a good bit of precedent there, and John didn't want to go back to ten furlongs [for the International Stakes].

'Bearing in mind the main target has always been the Arc, we think this is the best route.'

John Gosden, not taking victory in the Yorkshire Oaks for granted, saying: 'I've seen enough upsets in my time at York, notably Brigadier Gerard getting turned over by Roberto in the International, so we're not getting carried away.'

The trainer need not have worried as Jack Haynes reported:

Racing royalty Enable enjoyed the perfect Arc aperitif and enhanced her reputation as one of the best mares in history with a terrific tenth top-level success in the Yorkshire Oaks.

Little more than six weeks before a historic hat-trick bid in the Qatar Prix de l'Arc de Triomphe, the John Gosden-trained Enable turned on the style in her inimitable way to defeat the world's top-rated filly Magical on what is likely to be her final start on British soil.

Gosden's attention immediately turned to the task of readying Enable for a final French foray on October 6, when she will bid to go one better than dual winner Treve, whose quest for a third Arc was thwarted in 2015 when she finished fourth behind Golden Horn.

Sky Bet shortened Enable to a best-priced evens (from 11-10) to win the Arc, with a host of firms going as short as 4-5. Under a largely hands-and-heels ride from Frankie Dettori, Enable achieved her joint-third highest Racing Post Rating of 127 in accounting for Magical by two and three-quarter lengths, with Gosden hopeful Khalid Abdullah's mare will be 'mighty tough' to beat if she is at the peak of her powers at Longchamp.

Enable peers out of her box at Clarehaven Stables in Newmarket in August 2019

The trainer said: 'She wasn't at her best in the Arc last year but if she goes back to the form she showed when she won the race at three, which she looked like she was showing today, then she'll be mighty tough to beat.

'You always have to watch out for the three-year-olds. Sottsass and Japan were brilliant recently and they're the ones we'll have to watch as they will be getting the weight.

'Enable has this amazingly competitive mind and a wonderful constitution. The only time she was beaten was when she was boxed in, but that's life. She's a wonderful racemare.'

It was a fourth triumph in the Yorkshire Oaks for Gosden. For Enable, it was a second win in three years in a race won in 2018 by the ill-fated Sea Of Class, who pushed Enable closest to defeat during her 12-race winning run when a short-neck second in last year's Arc.

Gosden said: 'It was a gorgeous performance. She cruised around and really quickened. She really turned it on and Frankie [Dettori] was not hard on her.'

On returning to a heaving winner's enclosure, Dettori applauded the crowd as the crowd applauded him and his star mare. A brief look to the skies preceded the famous flying dismount.

Dettori, with tears in his eyes, said: 'I love her so much. I haven't lost with her yet and we've won everything.

'She's amazing, uncomplicated, has great presence and a massive engine. Everybody doubts her but she just keeps on winning.'

Enable did it the hard way by making all but it looked anything but. Dettori peered between his legs on the turn into the home straight, and again half a mile out. When Magical and stablemate Lah Ti Dar came within a length, Enable went into another gear.

There was ten lengths back to third Lah Ti Dar at the finish and a further length and a half to Ballydoyle's second string South Sea Pearl, but all the attention deservedly went the way of the winner.

Dettori said: 'I let Magical come to me and when I kicked she put it to bed. Magical is no slouch but Enable felt tremendous.

'We wanted to do an exercise canter with the Arc in mind but having Magical here made a race of it as she's very solid. She had a very hard race in the King George so this was a fantastic performance.'

In winning a tenth top-level prize, Enable matched the tally of fellow Juddmonte great Frankel, who wowed the adoring York crowd when winning at this meeting on his penultimate start in 2012.

Teddy Grimthorpe, racing manager to Abdullah and chairman at York, said: 'The Yorkshire crowd is fantastic and so knowledgeable – it's so vital for racing to have these stars. The way she performs every time is something else. Everyone is so proud of her.'

It was not just racegoers who were left in awe with Aidan O'Brien – trainer of runner-up Magical who drifted to 20-1 (from 12) for the Arc with Sky Bet – providing a fitting description of Enable.

O'Brien said: 'Enable was unbelievable. We have a lot of options with Magical. We'll see how she is when we get her back but she might go to Leopardstown next month.'

The Irish Champion Stakes or Matron Stakes may well await for O'Brien's leading filly but there is surely only one magical ending for Enable. Roll on Longchamp.

Everyone connected with Enable was delighted as Andrew Wilsher reported:

She is adored by John Gosden, the apple of Frankie Dettori's eye and worshipped by her thousands of followers. But nobody knows Enable quite as personally as Imran Shahwani.

Enable is clear of Magical in the Yorkshire Oaks

The 34-year-old, Enable's groom, has looked after her, cared for her and prepared her for all her big days. He even has the honourable duty of riding her out at home each morning in Newmarket.

Witnessing her achieve a phenomenal tenth Group 1 victory in the Yorkshire Oaks, the man who knows her best was overcome with emotion.

'Enable is so very special to me,' Shahwani said. 'I'm lost for words, and it's incredible to see how special she is to everyone. Of course I will be sad when she retires but she has nothing left to prove. She's done it all, she's a superstar.'

A keen racing fan growing up in Pakistan, Shahwani moved to England 14 years ago in pursuit of his dream and was given a chance by Gosden.

But never in his wildest dreams could he have believed he would one day have the greatest mare in the world under his care. It is a reality about which Shahwani still has to pinch himself every day.

'It's incredible and I can't believe it,' he added. 'This is my first job in England, and I owe all this to Mr Gosden. He is a gentleman, and always looks after me as he does everyone.'

Lee Mottershead was among the excited throng on the Knavesmire:

It started about a furlong and a half from home. Suddenly, as if instructed by a conductor, the thousands of admirers in York's handsome grandstands began to fill the racecourse with the wonderful sound of heartfelt applause. A nagging anxiety had been lifted.

In its place a communal salutation carried Enable to the winning post and beyond. It was about the past and the present, for they were thanking an exceptional horse for what she had done on this and other days, but it was also about the future, for they were wishing her well ahead of the great mission still to come.

The betting had suggested this latest assignment represented little more than a penalty kick, but there was much more to the Yorkshire Oaks than that.

That would have been obvious to anyone who had seen Frankie Dettori in the morning.

Those who did reported he wanted to be alone. He was nervous, just as he had been before that epic King George. It was evident as he paced around the hotel grounds, separated from all but his thoughts, and then again when he spoke to John Gosden in the gym.

'John wasn't actually in the gym,' pointed out the trainer's wife Rachel Hood. 'Frankie called him. They were both nervous but they are also both so professional. John has to prepare her and him to do it.'

Unlike last year, when Enable only returned in September, this latest preparation has gone beautifully. Yet as she walked around the pre-parade ring, doubts were expressed by Cleethorpes betting shop worker Adrian Buttery.

'Does she look right?' he asked. 'I'm not so sure she does. I want Magical to win. I know you're not supposed to say that but the prices are wrong. I'm sorry, but they are.'

Norfolk's John Hallett was more hopeful but even within him there was the palpable sense of trepidation that seemed to pervade the course.

'She is one of the best horses I've seen in my lifetime,' he said. 'It would be nice to see her go out from Britain on a high. Was it the right thing to bring her here, though? I'm not sure. They didn't need to but I'm very pleased they did.'

So were we all. Following Enable's draining battle with Crystal Ocean many had believed she would go straight to Longchamp. She came back to York because Gosden felt it would help not hinder her prospects of becoming the Prix de l'Arc de Triomphe's first triple champion.

The chances of that now look ever stronger but there is surely little chance we will again see her compete in Britain, even though confirmation has not definitively been given by Khalid Abdullah's camp. This was almost certainly her home soil farewell. Dettori certainly felt that to be the case.

In the handicap that preceded the Yorkshire Oaks he had been beaten a head in to second.

That was in the mind of the man with the Geordie accent who, as Dettori entered the paddock behind a security guard, shouted: 'Forget about the last race, Frankie, forget about the last race.' The man need not have worried. The only race on Dettori's mind all day would have been this one.

It was a race in which Enable was exquisite and so, too, was her partner. Enable may have been a 1-4 shot but the fourrunner contest could have become unpleasantly tactical. Dettori ensured it could not by jumping his mount quickly out of the gates before allowing her to dictate and then dismiss. Gosden summed it up adroitly when observing: 'It was a gorgeous performance.'

Those were gorgeous words.

From Dettori the words were few and far between. He is famously emotional but Enablemakes him emotional in a different way. 'I'm

Frankie Dettori shows his gratitude to Enable's delighted groom Imran Shahwani after the Yorkshire Oaks

tearful,' he told ITV's Oli Bell, and he was, just as he was when emerging from the weighing room to receive his prize.

'How embarrassing,' he said. 'I was crying out of happiness and because it's the last time we're going to see her in England.' Just saying that left him choked once more. 'Don't start me again,' he said. 'It was amazing – and what a reception.'

The reception was indeed glorious and it was deserved. 'It's a horserace and in a horserace anything can happen,' said Hood. 'That's why when John saw her powering away it lifted his spirits – and everybody else's.'

Unless plans change, there will be no more chances for Enable to lift those spirits on a British racecourse, but we cannot be greedy. This marvellous mare has been allowed to race. She could have been retired as an Arc-winning three-year-old. Instead she continued and we grew to love and admire her. She has forged a special place in our racing lives and memories.

The collective wish is for one last memory to be created. Plenty of those who packed York's pre-parade ring, paddock and winner's enclosure will already have paid for an autumn trip to Paris, to where they will be carried by trains, planes and the dream of witnessing something that has never happened before.

In all likelihood, this was British racing saying au revoir to Enable. When the faithful flock to Longchamp, let us hope for a fitting and unforgettable goodbye.

BHA chief executive Nick Rust hands out Enable flags to racegoers at York

Her Yorkshire Oaks victory put Enable in exalted company as John Randall wrote:

Enable joined an elite club of only three fillies and mares trained in Britain and Ireland to win at least 12 races in succession since 1900 with victory in the Yorkshire Oaks.

The record in that category is held by the great Pretty Polly, who triumphed in the first 15 races of her career, followed by Irish champion Sweet Wall, who won her last 13.

Pretty Polly, perhaps the greatest filly or mare of all time, was the overall champion two-year-old of 1903 and landed the fillies' Triple Crown as well as the Coronation, Nassau and Park Hill Stakes in imperious style in 1904, but suffered a first defeat on her 16th start and her only visit to France.

Sweet Wall was placed in the Irish 1,000 Guineas and Irish Oaks in 1928, but was never beaten again. She took her last six races that season, culminating in the Irish Cambridgeshire under top weight of 9st 4lb, and won all her seven races as a four-year-old.

Enable was third on her reappearance as a three-year-old but has triumphed in all 12 of her starts since, becoming, uniquely, a dual King George and Arc winner, and also landing the Oaks, Irish Oaks, Breeders' Cup Turf and Eclipse. She achieved her highest Racing Post Rating of 129 in her first Arc.

The all-time record for the longest winning sequence by a filly or mare trained in Britain or Ireland is 17 by Alice Hawthorn in 1844-45, when she won her second Doncaster Cup.

The British and Irish record for either sex is held by Meteor, who came second in the 1786 Derby and won his next 21 races. That record is currently threatened by Altior, who has won his last 19.

The world record for the longest winning sequence by a filly or mare is held by Kincsem, the legendary Hungarian champion who was unbeaten in a career of 54 races throughout Europe (1876-79). Next in that category are recent Australian stars Winx, who won her last 33 races, and the undefeated Black Caviar, with 25 wins.

The overall world record is 56 wins in a row by Camarero in Puerto Rico between 1953 and 1955.

Enable was just getting better and better. Longchamp and the chance to make racing history was just around the corner.

RACING POST RATINGS VIEW – **PAUL CURTIS**

Enable may have faced a straightforward task but she ran up to her best performance this year to win the Yorkshire Oaks, giving Magical a bigger beating than in the Eclipse and Breeders' Cup Turf to return a Racing Post Rating of 127+.

Having had just three-quarters of a length to spare over Magical at Sandown and Churchill Downs, Enable showed her superiority in extending that margin by two lengths at York, running up to her King George form to give her rival the 4lb beating pre-race figures suggested.

This was an 11th straight 120+ RPR from Enable and she could yet get back to her three-year-old peak RPR of 129 but, given her dominance, it's hard to see anything pressing her to that level and it would likely take a wide-margin win in the Arc to see her improve on this year's figures.

Despite his defeat in the Juddmonte International, Crystal Ocean sits just in front of Enable at the top of the rankings, but the sex allowance that in theory proved crucial in Enable's neck success at Ascot last month would again see her top rated were they to meet and she is effectively the leading performer in the world.

Magical (123) looks to have run as well as ever following Enable home, although Lah Ti Dar clearly was not at her best when beating rank outsider South Sea Pearl by only a length and a half.

6377 **DARLEY YORKSHIRE OAKS (GROUP 1) (BRITISH CHAMPIONS SERIES) (F&M)** **1m 3f 188y**

3:35 (3:35) (Class 1) 3-Y-O+ **£241,017** (£91,375; £45,730; £22,780) **Stalls** Centre

Form				RPR
1-11	**1**		**Enable**[26] 5414 5-9-7 126 .... FrankieDettori 1 (John Gosden) *sweating; mde all: shkn up 2f out: rdn over 1f out: styd on strly* **1/4**[1]	127+
1122	**2**	*2¾*	**Magical (IRE)**[47] 4668 4-9-7 122 .... RyanMoore 4 (A P O'Brien, Ire) *trckd ldng pair: hdwy over 3f out: chsd wnr and cl up 2f out: rdn to chal over 1f out: drvn and kpt on same pce fnl f* **4/1**[2]	123
-163	**3**	*10*	**Lah Ti Dar**[53] 4430 4-9-7 113 .... WilliamBuick 2 (John Gosden) *trckd ldr: hdwy over 3f out: cl up over 2f out: sn rdn and one pce fr wl over 1f out* **11/1**[3]	107
4130	**4**	*1½*	**South Sea Pearl (IRE)**[4] 6263 3-8-12 101 .... SeamieHeffernan 3 (A P O'Brien, Ire) *hld up: a in rr* **100/1**	105

2m 29.9s (-3.30) **Going Correction** -0.05s/f (Good)
WFA 3 from 4yo+ 9lb **4** Ran SP% **109.3**
Speed ratings (Par 117): **109,107,100,99**
CSF £1.66 TOTE £1.10; EX 1.60 Trifecta £1.40.
Owner K Abdullah **Bred** Juddmonte Farms Ltd **Trained** Newmarket, Suffolk

TWELVE

PRIX DE L'ARC DE TRIOMPHE

Longchamp, October 6, 2019

Previous spread: Frankie Dettori ponders what might have been after Enable's defeat in the Prix de l'Arc de Triomphe at Longchamp in October 2019

3.05 *Qatar Prix de l'Arc de Triomphe (Group 1) (3yo+ No Geldings) (Turf)* **ITV**
Winner £2,573,873.87 **1m4f**

£4504504.50 guaranteed **For** 3yo+ entires & fillies **Weights** 4yo+ entires 9st 5lb (59.5kg); 4yo+ fillies & mares 9st 2lb (58kg); 3yo colts 8st 13lb (56.5kg); 3yo fillies 8st 9lb (55kg) **Allowances** fillies and mares 3lb/4lb (1.5kg) **Entries** 81 **Confirmed** 12 **Penalty value 1st** £2,573,873.87 **2nd** £1,029,729.73 **3rd** £514,864.86 **4th** £257,207.21 **5th** £128,828.83

36-1111 **FRENCH KING** 56 — 4 9-5
1 (5) *ch c French Fifteen-Marina Piccola* — **Olivier Peslier**
H-A Pantall H H Sheikh Abdulla Bin Khalifa Al Thani — (127)

55-1331 **WALDGEIST** 21 — 5 9-5
2 (3) *ch h Galileo-Waldlerche* — **Pierre-Charles Boudot**
A Fabre Gestut Ammerland & Newsells Park — (135)

1/1-131 **GHAIYYATH (IRE)** 35 — 4 9-5
3 (12) *b c Dubawi-Nightime* — **William Buick**
Charlie Appleby (GB) Godolphin — (137)

325-223 **KISEKI (JPN)** 21 — 5 9-5
4 (7) *b/br h Rulership-Blitz Finale* — **Christophe Soumillon**
Katsuhiko Sumii (JPN) Tatsue Ishikawa — (129)

141-681 **BLAST ONEPIECE (JPN)** 49 — 4 9-5
5 (4) *b c Harbinger-Tsurumaru Onepiece* — **Yuga Kawada**
Masahiro Otake (JPN) Silk Racing Co Ltd — (132)

121-213 **FIEREMENT (JPN)** 49 — 4 9-5
6 (2) *b c Deep Impact-Lune d'Or* — **Christophe-Patrice Lemaire**
Takahisa Tezuka (JPN) Sunday Racing Co Ltd — (132)

44-1323 **NAGANO GOLD** 42 — 5 9-5
7 (11) *b h Sixties Icon-Never Enough* — **Mickael Barzalona**
Vaclav Luka Jr (CZE) Syndikat V3J — (129)

111-111 **ENABLE** 45 — 5 9-2
8 (9) *b m Nathaniel-Concentric* — **Frankie Dettori**
John Gosden (GB) K Abdullah — (140)

1112221 **MAGICAL (IRE)** 22 — 4 9-2
9 (8) *b f Galileo-Halfway To Heaven* — **Donnacha O'Brien**
A P O'Brien (IRE) Derrick Smith & Mrs John Magnier & Michael Tabor — (135)

1-43111 **JAPAN** 46 — 3 8-13
10 (10) *b c Galileo-Shastye* — **Ryan Moore**
A P O'Brien (IRE) Derrick Smith & Mrs John Magnier & Michael Tabor — (133)

252252 **SOFT LIGHT (FR)** 42 — 3 8-13
11 (6) *b c Authorized-Light Saber* — **Yutaka Take**
J-C Rouget Claudio Marzocco — (122)

41-5111 **SOTTSASS (FR)** 21 — 3 8-13
12 (1) *ch c Siyouni-Starlet's Sister* — **Cristian Demuro**
J-C Rouget White Birch Farm — (128)

2018 (19 ran) **Enable** (6) John Gosden 4 9-2 EvensF — Frankie Dettori RPR122

BETTING FORECAST: 8-11 Enable, 6 Japan, 7 Sottsass, 11 Ghaiyyath, Magical, 14 Waldgeist, 33 Blast Onepiece, Fierement, 40 French King, 66 bar.

THERE WAS ONLY one thing on the mind of Enable's connections following her second victory in the Yorkshire Oaks and that was an attempt at a historic third success in the Prix de l'Arc de Triomphe.

Enable carried the best wishes of former trainer Criquette Head, who came within touching distance of racing history when Treve's bid for three in a row came up short in 2015.

'I've never been under much pressure, to tell you the truth, and Treve came into the race unbeaten that year, so had every chance except we came up against a champion horse in Golden Horn, that's all,' she recalled.

In the week of the Arc Julian Muscat spoke to Rory Mahon, a stalwart of Juddmonte's Ferrans Stud who helped put Enable and Frankel on the road to greatness.

Rory Mahon isn't very good at feigning indifference. As a yearling colt by Sea The Stars stands before him, he outlines the bay's attributes in matter-of-fact tones. 'Good limbs, great temperament, a quick learner, very relaxed,' he says. But the longer his eyes linger, the harder it becomes for Mahon to contain himself.

His voice lowers an octave and he says with feeling: 'A beautiful colt. Everything about him is right. We've just started breaking him, and with no setbacks you can nearly guarantee he'll be one of the first to go into training in January.'

The colt is then long-reined into an indoor school, where he is put through his paces by head lad Dave Cottrell. By now Mahon's enthusiasm is infectious. 'A horse like him would be on your mind the whole time when he is out at exercise,' he says.

'You'd be watching him, making sure it wasn't getting to him mentally, looking all the time for signs of lameness. You couldn't help focusing on him and probably another 15 like him who are here on the farm. His dam Concentric is throwing some beautiful animals.'

Mention of Concentric lends poignancy to Mahon's words. Concentric is the dam of Enable. Like her Sea The Stars half-brother,

Rory Mahon next to a portrait of Frankel at Ferrans Stud, where he was manager for more than 40 years

Enable was broken and pre-trained at Prince Khalid Abdullah's Ferrans Stud, in County Meath, before she was sent into training with John Gosden in 2016.

So too was Frankel before he joined Sir Henry Cecil in 2010. The vast majority of Abdullah's 110 homebred Group 1 winners have been through Mahon's hands. He isn't so sentimental as to see them as his children, but where Concentric's progeny are concerned he is entitled to a sense of fatherly pride.

Until he stood aside in January, Mahon, 71, had managed Ferrans since 1973. In 1975 he foaled down Enable's fourth dam Fleet Girl. Ten years later, by which time Abdullah had bought the farm, he supervised the breaking of Fleet Girl's daughter Bourbon Girl, and subsequently Bourbon Girl's daughter Apogee – to be followed, in turn, by Apogee's daughter Concentric.

It's no wonder he is smitten by Concentric's Sea The Stars yearling, who is smaller than Enable was at the same stage. So is Concentric's unraced two-year-old filly by Frankel, who is due to join Gosden in early 2020. Named Portrush, she is also at Ferrans. As we catch up with her Mahon makes no effort to conceal his admiration.

Rory Mahon and groom Danny McCarthy tend to Portrush, a half-sister to Enable who later got off the mark at the second attempt at Yarmouth in July 2020

'She had a little setback in the spring, which is why she is still here,' he says. 'She's just starting back and will be nearly ready to race when she arrives with John. She's more forward than Enable was. I hope we'll be reading about her in the papers next year.'

For nearly 40 years Ferrans has been the domain of Juddmonte's homebred yearlings. Abdullah bought the farm in 1982 as part of a package including land, mares, foals and stallion shares from Dr Herbert Schnapka, a German oilman whose dreams of producing top-class thoroughbreds foundered on his divorce.

Schnapka's decade-long involvement had seen Ferrans consign sales-toppers at yearling sales. Fortuitously, however, the aforementioned Fleet Girl failed to make her reserve when Mahon took her to the sales in 1976. Mahon still has the catalogue – she went through as lot 199.

Mahon smiles wryly at the memory. The smile barely leaves his lips thereafter as he reflects on the 37 years he worked for Abdullah. In that time he has come to represent a Juddmonte institution, a man central to its success.

He is a stud manager of the old school, less happy in the office than out on the farm, and not at all afraid to get his hands dirty. Yet

A yearling Sea The Stars colt and half-brother to Enable who was later second on his debut at Ascot in September 2020

one thing sets him apart. Many of his ilk are stockmen whose sole concern is the wellbeing of their horses, but Mahon loves his racing. He knows that the racecourse is the proving ground for the work he does at home. Winning is the only litmus test.

Mahon remembers the young Enable for the fact she went through the breaking-in process smoothly. Although she was big and backward she was unlikely to run before the autumn of her two-year-old season, Enable's willingness to accept instruction and riders on her back meant she was among the first batch of Juddmonte's 2014 homebred crop to be sent into training.

'Everything was right with her at the time,' Mahon recalls. 'Her action was good, she moved very well and she was good-tempered, so she joined John Gosden in February of her two-year-old year.

'At that stage you knew she would improve a lot between two and three,' for the trainer to get these horses into their routine, their system. The sooner they are there the quicker the trainer can identify what they have. It takes trainers longer if the horses have to catch up.'

Enable made a winning debut at Newcastle in November 2016, but Mahon chuckles at what happened next. The subsequent winner of four Oaks, two King Georges and a Breeders' Cup Turf in addition to those two Arcs was the stable's second string when she reappeared at three in a conditions event at Newbury. Shutter Speed, another Juddmonte homebred, was Dettori's chosen mount and she duly obliged, with a considerately-ridden Enable closing late into third place.

'It's history now but at the time word came back to us that Shutter Speed was the better filly,' Mahon recalls. 'But Shutter Speed was more forward. She was on her game that day but she didn't progress, whereas Enable did. The secret was that John gave Enable time. If she was wrongly handled at that stage I doubt she'd be racing at five.'

Mahon has witnessed similar twists of fortune for himself. At Ferrans the main colts' yard has 25 boxes arranged in a square, into which Mahon puts the yearlings he feels are the pick of the crop. However, once the breaking process starts in September, it isn't unusual for the best horse to emerge from the other 25 who dwell in the yard's shadow.

'Come February, when you've got more work into them and they're stronger, you might ask yourself "How in the name of God did I ever put this colt in the second yard?" 'I'd remember very well why he might not have stood with the others in the beginning. He might not have walked so well, or maybe he turned his front feet out a little. But none of those are reasons why he should not be a racehorse. You can never be absolutely sure of anything. That's what has made the journey so exciting.'

It's surprising to learn that Mahon's parents were not horse people even though he wanted to do nothing else from a young age. He counts his blessings for having been in the right places at the right times, but as with his assessment of Abdullah's fortunes, you make your own luck in life.

'I have worked for the prince for most of my life,' he says. 'The first time I met him in 1982 he was extremely interested in the place he had just bought. He was clear that he wanted somewhere where his young horses were broken and pre-trained.

'He's a brilliant man on pedigrees and a hands-on boss. When he comes here he analyses every detail about each horse while looking at his stud book. He's never in any hurry, which is a wonderful thing with horses, and he loves his homebreds.'

The only rival Enable has in Mahon's affections is Frankel. 'It has been the thrill of my lifetime to be involved with Frankel and Enable, both of whom have won ten Group 1 races,' he says. 'To have lived through that is a dream. The two of them are such outstanding horses that you find yourself forgetting the others.'

Mahon was at Ascot when Frankel closed his career by winning the 2012 Champion Stakes, with Abdullah present. 'It was great to see the boss so excited,' he recalls. 'He's put so much into it and deserves the satisfaction he gets from big days like that.'

Of the young Frankel, Mahon says: 'He was a completely different character here than when he went to Sir Henry Cecil. He was a little free in training. Here he would walk to the gallop, do his canter, walk home, eat and sleep.

'When you looked over his box door at midnight he was always fast asleep. He was an extraordinary horse to be involved with – he was with you mentally every day and always very relaxed. He never had a vet near him, nor was he ever sick or lame. You'd nearly never notice him in the string except for that presence he had.'

Mahon may have stood aside as stud director, to be replaced by his son Barry, but Ferrans is now part of his genetic make-up. He no longer lives on site – Barry now occupies the house, just inside the main gates, where he and his three siblings were born. A Ferrans without Rory roaming the pastures is unthinkable, however.

'I will always be around the place,' he says. 'Someone asked me when I was going to retire and I'm the longest-serving of Juddmonte's employees. The prince and I are the only ones to be involved with four generations of Enable's family. I still feel like I'm 25 and enjoy it here as much as the first day I started.

'A lot of people put a lot of work into the game but don't get much out of it. The light might not shine so bright for them, but Juddmonte gets better and better every year. It's brilliant to be part of that, even a small part.'

So how will he feel when Enable's Sea The Stars half-brother walks into the horsebox that will take him across the Irish Sea to Gosden's stable. Will he feel a little lament? 'The thing about it is that you have a new dream every year,' Mahon says. 'When you send a bunch away, you always have the next ones coming up. That's the joy of it. Then you switch on the television and see these horses winning Group 1 races. How could you ever tire of that?'

The stage was set for Enable to make history at Longchamp, but as Lewis Porteous reported she was denied by the Andre Fabre-trained Waldgeist:

They cheered Enable leaving the parade ring, they cheered her leaving the stalls, they cheered her hitting the front and they even cheered her back to her stable, but when it mattered most there were no cheers.

Instead, there was a numbing silence as Waldgeist flashed past the winning post in front of Europe's darling to deny her a never-before-achieved third win in the Qatar Prix de l'Arc de Triomphe.

Nestled on the western edge of Paris's 16th arrondissement under the distant gaze of the Eiffel Tower, Longchamp has been the stunning backdrop to some remarkable Arcs, but there was a unique atmosphere both before and after the race's 98th running.

John Gosden and his wife Rachel Hood go to saddle Enable before the Arc

Fans arrived in their droves to witness Enable's quest for history, but the winner of her last 12 races, including ten at Group 1 level and the previous two Arcs, uncharacteristically wilted in the final furlong to suffer the same fate as Treve, the only other dual Arc winner who tried for the hat-trick but ultimately failed in 2015.

On that occasion Frankie Dettori pooped the party aboard Golden Horn but the tables were dramatically turned four years on as the Italian was left to suffer as Waldgeist showed a remarkable turn of foot to leave Enable in his wake.

'I struggled in the first bit of the race and let her find her feet,' said Dettori, dejected but in control of his emotions. 'She came good for me in the false straight and I waited for the 300 (a furlong and a half out) but I didn't find as much as I thought I'd left and I just folded a little bit. The winner was too good for me today.'

The hallmark of Enable's remarkable career has been the way she sustains her winning burst, but this time her kick appeared to peter out much earlier than usual, bringing back memories of last year's desperate finish when she just held on from Sea Of Class after a troubled preparation. On this occasion she could not hold on.

'I passed the 200 and I was a spent force,' added Dettori. 'I think the ground had a lot to do with it.'

While Enable's rider considered what might have been, her trainer John Gosden exited the scene sharply, although not before congratulating the winning connections. He later concurred that the rain-soaked ground had been a significant factor.

'She's run a blinder and I'm thrilled with her performance,' said Gosden. 'We lost our most potent weapon, the turn of foot in the latter stage of the race but I'm very proud of her.'

Rather than Enable, the history maker turned out to be winning trainer Andre Fabre, scoring a record eighth Arc win with a horse meeting Enable for the fourth time and beating her for the first.

Yet to beat Enable, with a horse who had trailed her home in last year's Arc, the Breeders' Cup Turf as well this year's King George, has to be one of his greatest achievements.

'I have so much admiration and respect for Enable that I'm proud Waldgeist could beat her,' said the 73-year-old, securing his 30th trainers' title in France with this victory.

Beaten 13 and a quarter lengths by Enable in America, Waldgeist finished just a length and three-quarters behind her at Longchamp 12 months ago.

However, it was at Ascot in July, after Waldgeist finished strongly to close to within two lengths of his old rival, that his trainer, and especially winning rider Pierre-Charles Boudot – scoring in the Arc for the first time – first thought an upset possible.

'He pleased me very much at Ascot and he's stronger and more mature,' added Fabre. 'I really thought he was eating the ground at Ascot and had an easy race, so it gave me some confidence.'

John Gosden was typically generous in defeat as Jonathan Harding reported:

John Gosden saw the sucker punch coming but neither he nor the collective will of the Longchamp crowd could change the very soft ground that hampered Enable in her bid for a historic third Arc.

The champion trainer was a figure of calm in a packed parade ring before the race despite carrying a heavy burden of expectation, and was equally composed when delivering his post-race analysis. Despite the difficult conditions, Gosden was pleased with Enable's run despite the difficult conditions and said a decision on the five-year-old's future would be made by owner Prince Khalid Abdullah in the coming days.

He was also full of praise for Waldgeist, who he felt simply stayed on best in the testing ground.

'She was beaten by a class horse who Andre has been pleased with this year. The winner just outstayed her in the rain,' said Gosden.

'Had it been good to soft I'd have been disappointed with finishing second but I saw the sucker punch coming. When I walked the course with Frankie [Dettori] and saw how far the stick was going in, I thought "Houston, we've got a problem".

'Enable has a great turn of foot with 400 metres to go but that was blunted in the ground. Her stamina gave out in an intense race over that trip. It's as simple as that. There was no hiding place.

'I can deal with the disappointment because she was fine after the race and I have a lot of respect for the winner and connections. We were beaten by a better horse on the day in the conditions.'

Enable was welcomed back into the parade ring to a chorus of cheers from the crowd and Gosden added: 'It was a lovely reception and it's great for racing. I'm sorry we didn't quite pull it off.'

#EnableChallenge
HIPPODROME PARISLONGCHAMP · 6 OCTOBRE 2019

8

Previous spread: Fans cheer Enable before she goes to post in the Arc

While they could not add another winning entry to Enable's fairy-tale story, Teddy Grimthorpe, racing manager to Khalid Abdullah, praised the star mare and her contribution to the sport.

'The expectation was enormous and the wave of goodwill was unbelievable,' said Grimthorpe. 'It's not quite what we hoped for but how can we complain? She's an unbelievable filly and we love her to death – we don't love her any less now.

'She's been very special to a lot of people and hasn't let us down. She's run a fantastic race and just got outstayed on the ground. We'll get her back, see how she is and contemplate a special filly.

'She's a fourth generation Juddmonte-bred, so an awful lot of people have been involved in the raising of the families so it's been hugely emotional and an exciting run. It's just extraordinary.'

Lee Mottershead was at Longchamp to witness Enable's history bid:

At the hands of the man they call Little Napoleon, Enable met her Waterloo. It was an exhausting, gruelling, heartbreaking battle, and it was a battle she lost, but the reputation of a racehorse can be bolstered in defeat as well as victory. If you had not believed that before the 98th running of the Prix de l'Arc de Triomphe, you surely do now.

When Frankie Dettori sent Enable into the lead just after the two-furlong pole it looked as though those present at Longchamp were set to see a most wonderful piece of history made before their eyes. With 200 metres to run she was clear. With 100 metres to run she was clear. At the winning post she was no longer clear. Instead she was a length and three-quarters behind Waldgeist. Andre Fabre had done it again.

They had met three times before. On each and every occasion Waldgeist had been humbled by Enable, first in last year's Arc, then in the Breeders' Cup Turf and most recently at Ascot, where France's challenger had finished an honourable third in the war of attrition that was the King George. The score was three-nil in Enable's favour, yet not only did Fabre try again, he did so with confidence. Fabre is a genius and now a genius with eight Arcs to his name.

Dettori has six and must wait until he is at least 49 before trying to make that seven. Some in his entourage had described him as 'nervous-excited' during the days that preceded a race in which Enable was seeking to do something that had never been done before. The still dual Arc heroine could not do it but in defeat she drained every last drop.

Whether British, Irish or French, the majority of those who came to Longchamp would surely have wanted Enable to win, in no small part so they could report having been here for a unique racing moment. There were Enable banners, scarves, bags and even reusable eco cups.

Mostly, there were Enable fans who cheered loud when, during the pre-race parade the racecourse commentator announced: 'Et maintenant, le champion, numero huit, Enable.' On hearing those words, and the reception they triggered, Dettori smiled and stroked the horse he loves more than he has loved any in his long career.

That career has been very long indeed. This was Dettori's 31st Arc, his first having been way back in the Tony Bin year of 1988 when among the jockeys riding against him were the victorious John Reid, Pat Eddery, Willie Carson, Walter Swinburn and Cash Asmussen. They were all stars but Dettori has become a bigger star, famous the world over, so famous that when the stalls crashed open a group of supporters began singing, 'Oh, Frankie Dettori', to the tune now more associated with Jeremy Corbyn.

From the top of the grandstand that chant was easy to hear, as was the groan that swept through the custard-coloured structure when, 50 metres from the line, Waldgeist galloped past Enable.

On his back was Pierre-Charles Boudot, who at the top of the home straight could have chosen to follow the favourite as Dettori struck for home. Rather than doing the obvious he briefly took a pull and steered Galileo's son around Sottsass and Japan. By doing so Waldgeist was wide of Enable when launching his attack, although that made no difference for Enable had no more to give. She had given her all.

At a time when most of us had hoped to see Dettori parading Enable in front of the enclosures he was actually bringing her back into the paddock, where enormous, appreciative cheers greeted their return.

There was no flying dismount but nor was there a crying dismount. Dettori saluted those who were saluting him and his girl. Then he kissed her on the neck, got off her back and explained that his darling had a been spent force passing the 200-metre pole. He had just endured what must have been a crushing experience yet he spoke frankly and graciously, as did John Gosden and Teddy Grimthorpe. All three were as admirable and impressive as their horse in defeat.

From atop the horse who beat them Boudot put his hands to his ears as Waldgeist entered the winner's circle. It looked like a plea for his partner to receive the credit he deserved, and while the five-year-old will not be remembered as a vintage Arc victor - he has lost more races than he has won - he more than deserved his applause. His triumph also delivered a slice of irony, for he was once part-owned by Coolmore, an operation that quite rightly spent three years trying to beat Enable but sold their interest in the horse who eventually did.

That horse won an Arc staged on jumping ground and in which the distances dividing the 12 runners were more akin to a winter jumps affair. This was wholly appropriate, for Boudot hails from a jumping family and Fabre once enjoyed enormous success both riding and training over jumps. Those days are now decades in the past.

Fabre long since established himself as the greatest French Flat trainer there has ever been. He is a brilliant man and a principled man, one who has consistently refused to run his Breeders' Cup raiders on raceday medication. In words and deeds he is one to whom all those entering his profession should aspire.

To see a thoroughbred win three Arcs remains an aspiration unfulfilled. It is perfectly possible that in our lifetimes no horse will again attempt the feat, let alone achieve it. The second horse to try came agonisingly close but, to collective disappointment, it was not to be.

'We don't love her any less,' said Grimthorpe as he looked at the valiant but vanquished heroine. We do not. At the scene of her Waterloo, we appreciated her even more.

Enable may have been beaten in her quest to make racing history, but she emerged from the Arc with her legacy intact as Tom Kerr reported:

In the end, it was not to be. The Prix de l'Arc de Triomphe will reach its centenary in 2020 without ever yielding a triple winner after Enable, worn down by a hard race on gruelling ground, was caught in the final yards by the Andre Fabre-trained Waldgeist.

The result silenced the British, Irish and French racegoers who had packed out Longchamp hoping – expecting – to witness Enable's march into history. They went home deflated, but most, like Enable's connections, would have been phlegmatic about it. Racing aficionados are familiar with the feeling of glory thwarted. This is not the first time racing's innate unpredictability has spoiled the script.

If this was Enable's swansong, she leaves the turf with her reputation entirely intact. Over the past three years she has met every challenge and, until this day, conquered every foe. In the process, she has earned a legion of admirers and achieved the sort of stature no British Flat horse has boasted since Frankel.

And the essential fact remains that what Enable was attempting to do stretched the boundaries of credulity. To win one Arc is a triumph – to win three on the trot would have been to overcome odds so long that only one horse in the race's 99-year history had even attempted the feat before.

That is perhaps the keenest agony from Longchamp: the knowledge that we will likely wait many moons to see another come along with the talent, durability and – above all – luck to try again. Enable had the talent, had the durability, but, at the last, her luck finally deserted her. Ultimately, she was likely undone by a few early-morning Parisian rain showers. C'est la vie.

Of course, perhaps the most potent force preventing the feat that eluded Treve and Enable being achieved by another is the economics of racing.

The lure of the breeding shed is such that those horses who have the potential to scale the heights will likely be retired long before the limits of their talent are truly tested.

That Enable was granted the opportunity to attempt something epoch-defining is something to celebrate, even if at final reckoning it proved a challenge too far, for in the undertaking she became exactly the sort of heroine this sport needs. By attempting something unprecedented, she captured the imagination and won the hearts of racing fans in three countries.

And while those who came from far and wide to cheer Enable went home deflated, there should be no sadness, no sense of failure. We thought Enable's destiny was to be the first horse to win three Arcs. Instead, this great champion will be remembered as only the second to try. That, on reflection, is a legacy to cherish.

Ten days after that agonising defeat, racing received the news it wanted when it was revealed that Prince Khalid had given Enable the go-ahead to remain in training as a six-year-old. She was later crowned Cartier Horse of the Year for a second time, matching the feat of the legendary Frankel, who also picked up the prize twice.

Enable's season in 2020 would be planned around a return to Longchamp for a second attempt to win the Arc for the third time. Before that, though, the world was shocked to its core by the coronavirus pandemic.

RACING POST RATINGS VIEW – **SAM WALKER**

Waldgeist rates an average winner of the Prix de l'Arc de Triomphe with a Racing Post Rating of 128 after getting the better of Enable by just under two lengths.

He sits between Workforce (130) and Golden Horn (127) among the recent colts to win the race, with all the other winners from the last decade being fillies.

The most obvious analysis angle on the race is that the pace collapsed notably in the closing stages (13.1 seconds for the last 200 metres), with favourite Enable unable to keep up her gallop on the very soft ground.

The John Gosden-trained mare would not have any trouble staying the distance on this ground in normal circumstances but Ghaiyyath took them along just a shade too fast for the conditions.

Ghaiyyath, Magical and Fierement set the pace and all underperformed by at least a stone on RPRs and Enable, who raced fourth, did well to hang on as long as she did.

Enable slowed down in the final furlong of last year's Arc before hanging on to win and, to his credit, Frankie Dettori timed it right to beat every horse bar the winner.

Waldgeist had raced a little further back and travelled strongly turning into the straight. In what was a gruelling slog to the line he simply slowed down slower than the rest, bagging trainer Andre Fabre his first Arc success since 2006.

This was a form reversal from the King George VI and Queen Elizabeth Stakes at Ascot, when he finished two lengths behind Enable in third.

Waldgeist has been found wanting at the highest level in recent years, having lost five of his previous six starts at Group 1 level, but he has been improving on RPRs this year and perhaps the conditions and pace just fell right for him to post this career-best performance.

Enable came agonisingly close to recording a third Arc success, but with two Arcs and two King Georges in the bag she remains one of the greatest middle-distance talents we have ever seen.

7941a **QATAR PRIX DE L'ARC DE TRIOMPHE (GROUP 1) (3YO+) (GRANDE COURSE) (TURF)** **1m 4f**

3:05 3-Y-O+ **£2,573,873 (**£1,029,729; £514,864; £257,207; £128,828)

Pos	Dist	Horse	Jockey / Draw	RPR
1		**Waldgeist**^{21} 7251 5-9-5 0 (A Fabre, France) *hld up towards rr of midfield: rdn and hdwy fr over 2f out: swtchd to outside 1 1/2f out: styd on wl to ld 50yds out: rdn out* **131/10**	Pierre-CharlesBoudot 3	128
2	*1 ¾*	**Enable**^{45} 6377 5-9-2 0 (John Gosden) *in tch: trckd ldrs 3f out: rdn to ld 2f out: drvn 1 1/2f out: hdd 50yds out: sn no ex* **1/2**^{1}	FrankieDettori 9	123
3	*1 ¾*	**Sottsass (FR)**^{21} 7253 3-8-13 0 (J-C Rouget, France) *in tch in midfield: hdwy to chse ldrs appr 2f out: sn rdn: drvn and kpt on same pce fr 1 1/2f out* **66/10**^{2}	CristianDemuro 1	123
4	*½*	**Japan**^{46} 6354 3-8-13 0 (A P O'Brien, Ire) *hld up towards rr of midfield: rdn and hdwy on outside fr under 3f out: chsd ldrs 1 1/2f out: sn drvn: kpt on same pce* **9/1**^{3}	RyanMoore 10	123
5	*6*	**Magical (IRE)**^{22} 7219 4-9-2 0 (A P O'Brien, Ire) *chsd ldr: led gng wl 2 1/2f out: rdn and hdd 2f out: wknd 1 1/2f out* **19/1**	DonnachaO'Brien 8	109
6	*3 ½*	**Soft Light (FR)**^{42} 6522 3-8-13 0 (J-C Rouget, France) *dwlt: towards rr: pushed along and kpt on steadily fr 2 1/2f out: n.d* **85/1**	YutakaTake 6	107
7	*8*	**Kiseki (JPN)**^{21} 7251 5-9-5 0 (Katsuhiko Sumii, Japan) *towards rr of midfield: rdn under 3f out: wknd 2f out* **44/1**	ChristopheSoumillon 7	94
8	*4 ½*	**Nagano Gold**^{42} 6522 5-9-5 0 (Vaclav Luka Jr, Czech Republic) *in rr: rdn and plugged on fr 2 1/2f out: nvr in contention* **85/1**	MickaelBarzalona 11	86
9	*4 ½*	**French King**^{56} 6007 4-9-5 0 (H-A Pantall, France) *towards rr: eased whn btn 2f out* **41/1**	OlivierPeslier 5	79
10	*2 ½*	**Ghaiyyath (IRE)**^{35} 6771 4-9-5 0 (Charlie Appleby) *led: rdn under 3f out: hdd 2 1/2f out: wknd qckly 2f out: eased fr 1 1/2f out* **13/1**	WilliamBuick 12	75
11	*nse*	**Blast Onepiece (JPN)**^{49} 4-9-5 0 (Masahiro Otake, Japan) *midfield: rdn 3f out: lost pl 2 1/2f out: sn struggling* **58/1**	YugaKawada 4	75
12	*15*	**Fierement (JPN)**^{49} 4-9-5 0 (Takahisa Tezuka, Japan) *trckd ldrs: lost pl under 3f out: sn struggling: eased fr 2f out* **36/1**	Christophe-PatriceLemaire 2	51

2m 31.97s (1.57) **Going Correction** +0.775s/f (Yiel)

WFA 3 from 4yo+ 6lb **12** Ran SP% **120.4**

Speed ratings: **125,123,122,122,118 116,110,107,104,103 102,92**

PARI-MUTUEL (all including 1 euro stake): WIN 14.10; PLACE 1.60, 1.10, 1.70; DF 7.40.

Owner Gestut Ammerland & Newsells Park **Bred** The Waldlerche Partnership **Trained** Chantilly, France

THIRTEEN

KING GEORGE VI AND QUEEN ELIZABETH STAKES

Ascot, July 25, 2020

Previous spread: Enable and Frankie Dettori cruise to a record-breaking third success in the King George VI and Queen Elizabeth Stakes in front of an empty grandstand at Ascot in July 2020

3.35 RACE 6

King George VI And Queen Elizabeth Qipco Stakes (Group 1) (British Champions Series) (Class 1) **ITV**

Winner £226,840 (1m 3f 211y)**1m4f**

£400,000 guaranteed **For** 3yo+ (NOTE: horses will be eligible to run in this race provided that they have a current BHA Handicap Rating of 80 or higher at midday of the confirmation stage. Horses which do not qualify for a rating may also be eligible providing the BHA Handicapper is satisfied that the horse's racecourse performances up to and including the day before confirmation merit a provisional assessment of 80 or higher. Horses which have not run will not be eligible) **Weights** 3yo colts & geldings 8st 10lb; fillies 8st 7lb; 4yo+ colts & geldings 9st 7lb; fillies 9st 4lb **Entries** 8 pay £5000 **Penalty value 1st** £226,840 **2nd** £86,000 **3rd** £43,040 **4th** £21,440

0330-25 **1** (1) **ANTHONY VAN DYCK** (IRE) TTF 36 **BF D2 S2 F2** 4 9-7
b c Galileo-Believe'n'succeed [1]**Oisin Murphy**
A P O'Brien (IRE) Mrs J Magnier & M Tabor & D Smith (128)

1114-43 **2** (2) **JAPAN** TTF 20 **D1 S3 CD1** 4 9-7
b c Galileo-Shastye **Ryan Moore**
A P O'Brien (IRE) Smith/Magnier/Tabor/Matsushima (132)

/2301-3 **3** (4) **SOVEREIGN** (IRE) TTF 28 **D1 S1** 4 9-7
ch c Galileo-Devoted To You [1]**William Buick**
A P O'Brien (IRE) Mrs J Magnier & M Tabor & D Smith (124)

/1112-2 **4** (3) **ENABLE** TTF 20 **BF D8 S4 F2 CD2** 6 9-4
b m Nathaniel-Concentric **Frankie Dettori**
John Gosden K Abdullah (138)

2019 (11 ran) **Enable** (11) John Gosden 5 9-4 8/15F Frankie Dettori RPR127

BETTING FORECAST: 1-2 Enable, 11-4 Japan, 12 Anthony Van Dyck, Sovereign.

AS WINTER TURNED to spring and the pandemic hit Britain, Enable and the rest of the horse population were restricted to gallops duty as racing was shut down for 76 days. This didn't affect Enable as she would only begin her campaign midway through the season and in early June John Gosden said she would reappear in the Coral-Eclipse Stakes.

Gosden expected Enable to improve more for her comeback than in previous seasons as she attempted to become the first six-year-old to win the Eclipse since Bendigo won the inaugural running in 1886.

She finished second to Ghaiyyath, but as Lee Mottershead reported the Enable team were far from downhearted:

To say a race with the rich heritage and deserved prestige of the Coral-Eclipse does not matter would be wholly wrong but for the connections of Enable it mattered mostly this year because it served as a means to a far greater end.

Based on the evidence of Sandown, we and they are entitled to be no less hopeful of there being the happiest possible ending to an incredible story at Longchamp in October.

John Gosden is not Mystic Meg but he was impressive in forecasting the future when interviewed on ITV just minutes before Enable made her six-year-old reappearance.

Rarely can a tall man in a Panama hat have tried so hard to play down expectations. He had said Enable would need the run when she came to the Eclipse 12 months ago. Yes, she won that day, but this time she would really need the run.

Another year older, she has taken that bit longer to blossom and trim down, although Gosden, mindful not to embarrass the sport's leading lady, declined to publicly reveal her weight or daily pie consumption. He did give us a figure on her fitness - and 85 per cent was surely not going to be sufficient if Ghaiyyath performed. Aided by an excellent William Buick ride, Ghaiyyath really performed.

If ever a track was made for the Godolphin galloper, it was Sandown. Responding to Buick's requests, he went up and down the gears at exactly the right times. He also got down and dirty and grafted, which not everyone had believed he would, perhaps unfairly so, given Dubawi's son has delivered much more often than he has folded.

Had he not fancied a fight, Sandown's hill in a headwind would have provided mighty good reason to ease off, yet he fought, and so did Enable.

Gosden knows that at an age when Enable may well expect to be made a dame in the next honours list, the mighty mare is still up for it and keen to compete. The trainer was happy, Frankie Dettori was happy and Enable should have gone home happy, having been shown due respect from the saddle. Paris in the autumn is all-important, but when Enable returns to Ascot for the King George you can guarantee Gosden will not rate her readiness at 85 per cent.

At Ascot she took on – and routed – two rivals from Ballydoyle as Lewis Porteous reported:

An eerie silence greeted Enable at Ascot, similar to the one at Longchamp last October, but to the collective joy of her legion of fans the result could not have been more different.

They travelled in their droves to witness history being made in Paris only for Enable to come up agonisingly short in her quest for a third Prix de l'Arc de Triomphe, a result that stunned Longchamp into silence.

Her adoring fans were forced to watch from afar yesterday, but this time there was no disappointment as Enable galloped to where no thoroughbred has been before, becoming the first three-time winner of Ascot's midsummer showpiece, the King George VI and Queen Elizabeth Qipco Stakes.

This performance will not go down as her finest, but how could it when she was facing just two rivals? However, when connections finally call time on one of the most remarkable careers on turf, yesterday will be among the days that will define her legacy.

A race first run in 1951, only Enable, Dahlia and Swain had won the King George twice before yesterday, but she now stands alone after adding an unprecedented third success under an emotional Frankie Dettori.

'She touches my heart,' said the winning rider. 'I love her so much. She's taken me to emotional feelings and heights other horses haven't. I'm trying to enjoy her as much as all of us.'

There was palpable fear that the tactics of the first ever three-runner King George could overshadow the event, but there was no finer sight for Enable supporters than Dettori giving a long, lingering look over his shoulder with two furlongs to run.

Confident he had front-runner Sovereign covered, it was soon clear market rival Japan, sitting in third, was also cooked and from that moment it was all about Enable and her King George coronation.

'I couldn't believe it,' said Dettori as he relived that look over his shoulder. 'I thought, 'Where is he?' Everything was so quiet and I was surprised Japan was so far back and off the bridle.

'Enable was great today, she was like a hot knife through butter. It's a great feeling to have.

'It's never been done before – three King Georges – and I've a bit of a lump in my throat. I've only got her for two more months and I'm a bit emotional about it. She's special.'

A familiar path now awaits Enable, with York's Ebor meeting next month again set to provide the stepping stone to Paris in October and the quest for that elusive third Arc.

Had she been beaten here, that dream may have also been extinguished in the Ascot rain, but instead she marches on to Longchamp and, after ending a run of two consecutive defeats, Dettori believes again.

'She's not getting better but she is the same,' he said. 'She's thriving with racing. If she showed any sign of weakness going to the Arc would be a non-event.

'Three King Georges is amazing but the dream really is to win three Arcs. We came so close last year and, with this kind of performance, we're still in with a shot.

'If she was third today, you'd think scrap the idea and head for stud but at least we know we can be competitive.'

Paddy Power and Betfair Sportsbook cannot split Enable and three-year-old filly Love at the head of the Arc market, offering 3-1 the pair.

A tantalising dress rehearsal in the Yorkshire Oaks could be on the cards if Enable bids to win the mile-and-a-half race for a third time, although the Juddmonte International over shorter remains on the table.

'Love is a three-year-old and would get the weight [in the Yorkshire Oaks] but we took the benefit of that,' said winning trainer John Gosden.

'With Enable it could be a ground decision. If they got the rain and if the ground is soft, which it certainly can be at York, I would happily run in the Juddmonte International. If the ground is quick I would prefer to go over a mile and a half.'

Rather than tactics, Gosden revealed the timing of a heavy shower at Ascot had set his nerves jangling, but in the end he was left to savour another remarkable performance from the most remarkable mare he has ever had through his hands.

'The race went perfectly,' he said. 'We were a little concerned that the ground is pretty quick here and I'm always concerned when you get rain on quick ground that something might lose its hind legs on the bend, but luckily that didn't happen. She was quite imperious today.

'It was a small field but it was an elite field of Group 1 horses.'

After her 11th success at the top level, Enable now boasts three King Georges, an Oaks and Irish Oaks, two Yorkshire Oaks, two Arcs, a Coral-Eclipse and a Breeders' Cup Turf, but like Dettori it is that never-before-achieved third Arc that Gosden and owner-breeder Khalid Abdullah crave.

'He's an amazing owner and I've luckily trained for him for nearly 40 years,' said Gosden. 'He totally understands his horses and knows his pedigrees inside out. He clearly felt this was a filly who could do it again.

'It just slipped through our fingers last year – the winner beat us fair and square – but being the sportsman that he is and the great breeder he is he said, 'Let's go again'.

'I find the responsibility quite enormous and it weighs heavy, but what a pleasure to be around a racemare like her.'

We may have been here before, but the die is surely cast this time. Two races to go before the saddle probably comes off Enable's back for the last time. Roll on York and roll on Longchamp, where yet more history awaits.

Lee Mottershead was also on hand to witness another memorable performance:

It rained on her parade and it rained on her procession but Enable, the queen of the King George, still reigns. The only real sadness is so few people are able to say they got soaked seeing history made at Ascot.

Never before had only three runners contested the prize around which the summer of European Flat racing has for so long revolved.

Never before, though, had a horse won that magnificent showpiece three times.

If you like your glass half empty you will concentrate on the former fact. If you prefer a glass half full you will celebrate the latter fact. For so many reasons, both empirical and emotional, this was a day to celebrate.

Had there been a meaningful crowd here, ITV viewers may have missed out on what happened 13 seconds after Enable elevated herself above Dahlia, Swain and indeed all those turf greats who have won the King George VI and Queen Elizabeth Qipco Stakes. For with the grandstands silenced, save for the applause made by the lucky few, it was easy to hear Dettori scream: 'I love you!' It may not be possible for anyone to love Enable more than Dettori loves Enable, but racing fans all around the world will share his soppiness.

As the sport approached its emergence from shutdown, Dettori gave an interview to the Racing Post in which he revealed a level of devotion for a horse seldom expressed by a hardened professional. In short, he adores her. In short, she pulverised them.

It is true there were only two to pulverise but that is not her fault. It is, perhaps, nobody's fault. For although we can deliver doomsday predictions about what a three-runner King George says about the race, we should also place the disappointment in context.

This is the strangest of all Flat seasons, one in which the Derby and Oaks preceded Ascot's most coveted prize by just 21 days. With the exception of the Epsom champions, Ghaiyyath and perhaps Sottsass, it is hard to think of any star names who might have been obvious contenders for this 70th King George.

It is true John Gosden and Aidan O'Brien dominate the sport, particularly in the realm of middle-distance performers, but that was equally true 12 months ago when Enable beat ten opponents, including rivals trained in Britain, Ireland, France and Japan. The

Frankie Dettori treats the small number of people present in the Ascot winner's enclosure to a flying dismount to celebrate Enable's third King George victory

King George was not a failing race then and it is not a failing race now. It is simply one that over time has become slightly less coveted due to a series of external factors. Let us please not succumb to excessive melodrama.

Instead, let us bask in what we witnessed just after the two-furlong pole, at which point a still cantering Enable was eating into Sovereign's lead. Dettori pulled down a pair of goggles and then enjoyed a lingering look to his left. What he saw – albeit increasingly in the distance – was Ballydoyle's number-one hope Japan toiling in his mount's wake.

'I couldn't believe it,' said Dettori, before comparing the empty grandstands with the near emptiness behind him. 'Look, first of all there is nobody here. Then I thought: 'Where is he?' I was surprised he was so far back and off the bridle because he's a good tool. It's great. She was like a hot knife through butter.'

The knife stormed five and a half lengths clear. As the winning post was passed, Gosden made his way off the steppings, the shoulders of his raincoat saturated by the pouring rain. He had told us Enable was not ready to win the Eclipse and he had been quick to blame himself and Dettori for that agonising Longchamp defeat. Yet without that deflating day we would not have had this inspirational afternoon. We would not have a horse who could be the first to win both the King George and Arc on three occasions, a legend in pink, green and white.

'The girl is back!' screamed Dettori as he made his way to the now obligatory post-race Zoom conference. 'Good for the sport – and good for my wallet,' he gleefully pointed out and then displayed further delight when reminded he had equalled Lester Piggott's record of seven King George triumphs.

'Seven King Georges!' he declared. 'Can you imagine? I remember when the Queen gave me the trophy after one of my early ones. I was talking to her and said that it was my third or fourth King George. She turned around to me and said: 'Well, Lester won seven.' She put me straight back in my box. Well, now I've done it!'

He has done it and so has she, never more often than in a jewel of the turf that was referenced in the 1952 book, Homes Of Sport, penned by future ITV racing anchor John Rickman. Stressing that Ascot was not all about the royal meeting, he wrote: 'Each programme contains a centrepiece event which is well up to the level of Royal Ascot races. For instance, in July, 1951, there was the £30,000 King George VI and Queen Elizabeth Festival of Britain

Stakes, a race which if not in name has, in substance, come to stay.'

It has stayed, endured and entertained. Now, at last, the King George has its first triple winner.

'What a mare she has been,' said commentator Simon Holt as Enable approached the stalls. What a mare she has been and what a mare she remains. What a mighty, magnificent mare.

RACING POST RATINGS VIEW – **PAUL CURTIS**

With upwards of 7lb in hand of her rivals on their best form, Enable faced a straightforward assignment on the figures in her bid to land a third King George.

And despite the easy five-and-a-half-length success, Enable did not have to run to her best. A Racing Post Rating of 124+ falls 3lb shy of the mark she ran to when holding Crystal Ocean by a neck in a much stronger race last year. It's still a notable figure though, matching the level attained by the last older mare to win the race, Danedream in 2012.

This was clearly a step forward from the Eclipse, and at her best she's still very much the one to beat in the Arc with the performance suggesting last year's 128 is still attainable.

Notwithstanding Enable's historic success, the King George clearly lacked strength in depth with Sovereign's RPR of 118 good enough to have made the frame in only three of the past ten runnings. Assessed as having matched last year's front-running Irish Derby win, he had not managed to get within 10lb of that performance in any other run heading into the race and time will tell if he's worthy of it.

3661 **KING GEORGE VI AND QUEEN ELIZABETH QIPCO STKS (GROUP 1) (BRITISH CHAMPIONS SERIES)** **1m 3f 211y**

3:35 (3:35) (Class 1) 3-Y-O+ **£226,840 (**£86,000; £43,040) **Stalls** Low

Form					RPR
12-2	**1**		**Enable**[20] 2976 6-9-4 128 (John Gosden) *trckd ldr: gng best and led over 1f out: in the clr fnl f: easily* **4/9**[1]	Frankie Dettori 3	124+
01-3	**2**	*5 ½*	**Sovereign (IRE)**[28] 2656 4-9-7 117 (A P O'Brien, Ire) *led: 6 l ahd and pushed along 4f out: rdn 3f out: hdd over 1f out: sn no ch w wnr but styd on* **12/1**[3]	William Buick 4	118
4-43	**3**	*11*	**Japan**[20] 2976 4-9-7 122 (A P O'Brien, Ire) *trckd ldrs: rdn over 2f out: sn no imp: wknd and eased ins fnl f* **5/2**[2]	Ryan Moore 2	111

2m 28.92s (-3.68) **Going Correction** +0.075s/f (Good) **3** Ran SP% **105.5**

Speed ratings (Par 117): **115,111,104**

CSF £5.06 TOTE £1.20; EX 4.40 Trifecta £5.10.

Owner K Abdullah **Bred** Juddmonte Farms Ltd **Trained** Newmarket, Suffolk

FOURTEEN

PRIX DE L'ARC DE TRIOMPHE

Longchamp, October 4, 2020

Frankie Dettori gives Enable a pat after their sixth-place finish in the Prix de l'Arc de Triomphe at Longchamp in October 2020

3.05 pm *Qatar Prix de l'Arc de Triomphe (Group 1) (3yo+) (Grande Course) (No Geldings) (Turf)* **ITV**
Winner £1,452,711.86 **1m4f**

£2542372.88 guaranteed **For** 3yo+ **Penalty value 1st** £1,452,711.86 **2nd** £581,186.44 **3rd** £290,593.22 **4th** £145,169.49 **5th** £72,711.86

No. (Draw)	Form	Horse	Breeding	Trainer	Owner	Age	Wgt	Jockey	RPR
1 (7)	2-21141	**PERSIAN KING** (IRE) TTF 28	*b c Kingman-Pretty Please*	**A Fabre**	Godolphin Snc & Ballymore Thoroughbred Ltd	4	9-5	**Pierre-Charles Boudot**	133
2 (8)	563252	**ROYAL JULIUS** (IRE) 14	*b h Royal Applause-Hflah*	**J Reynier**	Jean-Jacques Biarese	7	9-5	**Shane Foley**	120
3 (6)	621215	**WAY TO PARIS** TTF 21	*gr h Champs Elysees-Grey Way*	**Andrea Marcialis**	Paolo Ferrario	7	9-5	**Ioritz Mendizabal**	127
4 (11)	14-4335	**JAPAN** TTF 22	*b c Galileo-Shastye*	**A P O'Brien (IRE)**	D Smith/Mrs J Magnier/M Tabor/M Matsushima	4	9-5	**Yutaka Take**	132
5 (10)	301-326	**SOVEREIGN** (IRE) TTF 21	*ch c Galileo-Devoted To You*	**A P O'Brien (IRE)**	Mrs J Magnier & M Tabor & D Smith	4	9-5	**Mickael Barzalona**	127
6 (14)	12-3112	**STRADIVARIUS** (IRE) TTF 21	*ch h Sea The Stars-Private Life*	**John Gosden (GB)**	B E Nielsen	6	9-5	**Olivier Peslier**	134
7 (4)	13-4124	**SOTTSASS** (FR) TTF 22	*ch c Siyouni-Starlet's Sister*	**J-C Rouget**	White Birch Farm	4	9-5	**Cristian Demuro**	132
8 (5)	112-211	**ENABLE** TTF 29	*b m Nathaniel-Concentric*	**John Gosden (GB)**	K Abdullah	6	9-2	**Frankie Dettori**	136
9 (12)	434-257	**DEIRDRE** (JPN) TTF 66	*b m Harbinger-Reizend*	**Mitsuru Hashida (JPN)**	Toji Morita	6	9-2	**Jamie Spencer**	127
10 (9)	25-2103	**GOLD TRIP** (FR) 21	*b c Outstrip-Sarvana*	**F Chappet**	Ecurie Jean-Louis Bouchard	3	8-13	**Stephane Pasquier**	119
11 (13)	6-33101	**CHACHNAK** (FR) 28	*b c Kingman-Tamazirte*	**F Vermeulen**	Ecuries La Vallee Martigny Earl & Des Mouettes	3	8-13	**Tony Piccone**	117
12 (1)	1312	**IN SWOOP** (IRE) 21	*b c Adlerflug-Iota*	**F-H Graffard**	Gestut Schlenderhan	3	8-13	**Ronan Thomas**	120
13 (3)	4-46131	**MOGUL** TTF 21	*b c Galileo-Shastye*	**A P O'Brien (IRE)**	M Tabor & D Smith & Mrs J Magnier	3	8-13	**Ryan Moore**	123
14 (15)	0-5114	**SERPENTINE** (IRE) TTF 21	*ch c Galileo-Remember When*	**A P O'Brien (IRE)**	Mrs J Magnier & M Tabor & D Smith	p3	8-13	**Christophe Soumillon**	130
15 (2)	11412	**RAABIHAH** (USA) TTF 21	*ch f Sea The Stars-Garmoosha*	**J-C Rouget**	Hamdan Al Maktoum	3	8-9	**Maxime Guyon**	125

2019 (12 ran) **Waldgeist** (3) A Fabre 5 9-5 131/10 Pierre-Charles Boudot RPR128

BETTING FORECAST: 11-10 Enable, 13-2 Stradivarius, 8 Sottsass, 10 In Swoop, 12 Mogul, 14 Japan, Raabihah, Serpentine, 16 Persian King, 50 Gold Trip, Sovereign, Way To Paris, 66 Deirdre, 100 Chachnak, Royal Julius.

ENABLE WOULD HAVE one more run before the Arc and in the middle of August connections revealed it would be in the September Stakes rather than the Yorkshire Oaks.

Following the York contest the Arc had a new favourite after the Aidan O'Brien-trained Love demolished her rivals. She had earlier landed the 1,000 Guineas and Oaks.

Enable then completed her racecourse preparations with a straightforward success at Kempton as Lee Mottershead reported:

If this was Enable's final outing on a British racecourse, it could hardly have gone better as the world's most famous racehorse teed herself up for a history-making trip to Paris with a performance that left John Gosden declaring: 'Game on!'

Gosden was adamant he did not want Enable to lock horns with Love in last month's Yorkshire Oaks, but following a predictably easy success in the Unibet September Stakes, the champion trainer, like all racing fans, is eagerly awaiting their showdown in the Qatar Prix de l'Arc de Triomphe.

'That was mission accomplished,' said Gosden, who watched from the running rail as Enable and Frankie Dettori repeated their 2018 victory in Kempton's most prestigious Flat race.

On that occasion Enable duelled up the home straight with the mighty Crystal Ocean. This time she was in a different league to the remaining five runners and proved that on the sand, making almost all the running to win unchallenged by seven lengths.

Indeed, the only moment of concern came when she was smacked under the chin by a stall's handler's rope. That caused her to begin slowly. She finished quickly.

'She had a go at kicking me saddling up, so it was important she had a race to take a little of that fizz out of her,' explained Gosden.

'It was very good for her mentally to have the race. She has had a nice blow, which we could have done at home, but you can't rehearse going to the racecourse.

'She has hopefully had a nice day out and it was a great to see her. It's a shame there wasn't a crowd here to see her but c'est la vie.'

Gosden will now hope la vie est belle when Enable meets Love at Longchamp on October's first Sunday, seeking to go one place better than when second last year in her bid to become the Arc's first triple winner.

'We have enormous respect for the Oaks winner,' said Gosden of Love.

'If Enable had gone to the Knavesmire I don't know who would have won but, my goodness, they would both have had a hard race – and I did not want her to have a hard race on the Knavesmire seven and a half weeks before the Arc. That wouldn't have been a clever way of getting there.

'You have seen how the French trainers do it. Look at Monsieur Fabre last year with Waldgeist. I learn from my friends.'

Enable has become one of Dettori's very best friends. He is desperate to claim his seventh Arc on Khalid Abdullah's mare, mainly because he knows it will be her third Arc.

John Gosden congratulates Enable and Frankie Dettori after their victory in the September Stakes at Kempton

'I'm not saying she is going to win, but we can still dream,' he said. 'It's possible. It's going to be tough against Love but we are in the mix.'

Enable and Frankie Dettori stretch out on the Limekilns round gallop in Newmarket on the Monday before the Prix de l'Arc de Triomphe

As Arc day approached and, with Enable completing her final preparations in Newmarket, conditions at Longchamp deteriorated. Testing ground was not expected to favour Love, so Enable replaced O'Brien's filly as favourite. This was despite very soft being in the going description 12 months earlier when Enable was reeled in late on by Waldgeist.

The horse who finished third behind Waldgeist and Enable, Sottsass, was described as 'better than ever at this stage of the season' by trainer Jean-Claude Rouget.

Frankie Dettori was desperate for Enable to join the greats by winning a third Arc. He said: 'It's more for her than for me. I want her to be remembered as one of the greats, and that will only happen if she wins a third Arc. I want her to be up there because I care about her.'

Gosden expressed his fears about the ground when he said: 'Defeat is a strong likelihood on this ground. I feel it has very much gone against her chances.'

It was all set up for a fascinating and intriuging contest, but there was one final twist in the tale. O'Brien revealed late on the Saturday night that all of his runners at Longchamp, including his four in the Arc, would be withdrawn after urine samples that were sent to a French lab returned positive for the prohibited substance Zilpaterol as a result of a batch of contaminated feed.

However, there was no fairytale third success for Enable as Lee Mottershead reported:

This year, as last year, Enable stood defeated in Longchamp's elegant paddock. Still on the racecourse where the daring dream had sunk in the mud was Sottsass. Soon he would return for a moment that summed up what sport is like.

Enable remains the most successful horse in the history of the Arc. Not, however, this Arc.

The hero of this hour was about to arrive. With Enable recovering exactly in the trajectory path that would take Sottsass into the winner's circle, a member of the security staff rushed over to the mare and groom Imran Shahwani.

'Okay, okay, let's go, let's go,' he said to Shahwani, shooing them away from the scene. A few seconds later she was gone. She will never be forgotten.

With less than 15 minutes until the start of the 99th Arc, one staged in front of just 1,000 spectators, hopes were still high Enable would become the first horse ever to conquer Flat racing's highest peak on three occasions.

The sense that fate had been smiling in her favour had strengthened on Saturday evening when a batch of contaminated feed resulted in Ballydoyle withdrawing their four intended Arc runners. Aidan O'Brien's loss was surely John Gosden's gain. Enable would not relish the conditions that had already claimed Love, but she had form on a testing track, including in past Arcs, and was now odds-on with pari-mutuel punters.

Frankie Dettori was waiting. Never before has he loved a horse like the one who won him his fifth and sixth Arcs. Here now was a chance to avenge last autumn's agonising defeat. With 31 Arcs behind him and a potentially seismic 32nd within touching distance, Dettori looked deep in concentration, alone with his thoughts. One heel was kicked against the other. Not long now.

In came Bjorn Nielsen, owner of Stradivarius, the stayer supreme normally partnered by Dettori but this time entrusted to Olivier Peslier. Nielsen brought the two riders together for a supportive but gentle hug.

Then it was the turn of Teddy Grimthorpe, racing manager to Enable's owner-breeder Khalid Abdullah. Like many of us Brits in Paris, Grimthorpe will be forced to spend 14 days in quarantine on his return home. No matter. He said he would have swum the channel to be here. Such was the rain in Paris prior to the weekend, he might at one point have needed to swim across the Bois de Boulogne as well.

The bell tolled for jockeys to mount. Between Grimthorpe and Dettori there was a fist pump. It proved not to be enough.

In this strangest of seasons it was the strangest of Arcs. Dettori said later he had wanted to go from the front. 'In the first 400 metres I was out of my comfort zone, so I left her,' he explained.

Instead Persian King, a Group 1-winning miler on his most recent start, was the unlikely leader, yet at nothing like the sort of pace Sovereign or Serpentine would have set. Most of us thought their absence would help Enable. In Gosden's opinion it turned out to be hindrance.

The pace was too slow, the ground too soft, although at the top of the home straight 'the queen' – the fitting description given to her by the racecourse commentators – still appeared to be cruising. Not for long.

As soon as Dettori asked a question two furlongs from home, Enable was beaten. Outsider Chachnak even tried to take a bite out of her. At no point did Dettori touch his six-year-old darling with the whip. To have done so in the circumstances would have seemed almost disrespectful.

'When I pressed the button nothing was there,' said Dettori. 'She couldn't pick her legs up in the ground, a bit like in the final furlong last year. It wasn't to be. I'm not emotional at the moment but I will be when I see her again. I'm still a bit angry because things didn't go my way – but we tried.'

The anti-climax was huge but Cristian Demuro quite rightly did not care. The roar he let out on passing the post might well have been heard at the real Arc de Triomphe. Groom Lea Metayer was in floods of tears. For her, this was all about her treasured horse winning, not Enable losing.

Enable (right) can get no closer than sixth as Sottsass claims the Arc

For most others that was not the case – and saying that is in no way disrespectful to Sottsass. It was inevitable that as we awaited the victor's arrival, our eyes should stay on Enable.

Just before dismounting, Dettori kissed her on the neck. He then remained at her side, passing on a few sweet nothings, lingering longer for a cuddle. Of all the sights so many were prevented from seeing in the flesh this year, these were the pictures you would have most remembered.

'He knows her and she knows him,' said Grimthorpe after the lovers had parted. He declined to retire her, for that decision rests with Abdullah, yet the hints were there.

'How can we ever be disappointed by her? She has given us so much,' stressed Grimthorpe. 'As I said to you last year, we do not love her any less.'

Nor do we. One hundred years after the Arc was born and in front of 1,000 spectators, we had yearned to salute a horse in a million. As Dettori had observed, it was just not to be.

To Sottsass, we offer congratulations. To Enable, with endless gratitude, we may well have said goodbye.

The final word on the 2020 Arc goes to Enable's trainer as Jonathan Harding reported:

John Gosden said a decision on Enable's future would not be made for at least a week after she was denied an unprecedented third Arc.

The six-year-old could manage only sixth in testing conditions at Longchamp, with the trainer putting her performance down to her not handling the ground as well as a lack of pace in the race.

'She seemed great afterwards,' said Gosden. 'It was sporting for Khalid Abdullah to allow her to come back and try again this year, and had she not she wouldn't have won another King George.

'We'll see what the plan is with her and whether she's retired immediately. As always, Prince Khalid will want a report on her a week after the race and we'll see what happens from there.

'She didn't have a taxing race because they didn't go a good old gallop like they do in England and Ireland, but that's horseracing. If you can't take the punches in this game you shouldn't be in it.'

Gosden said the late withdrawal of the Aidan O'Brien-trained runners on Saturday evening, including frontrunners Serpentine and Sovereign, had a notable impact on the tactics of the race.

'We knew Serpentine and Sovereign were key to the running of the race,' said Gosden. 'They would have set an even gallop and once they were withdrawn the whole complexion changed.

'There was a concern there would be no pace and Pierre-Charles Boudot set a modest one on Persian King. Enable is a mile-and-a-half filly who would have appreciated more speed to aim at.

'Frankie [Dettori] felt she was not happy with the deep, drying ground and that her action was not suited to it. That's the first time she's ever finished out of the first three in her life.

'It was the pace and the ground, it's as simple as that. It's not very complicated.

'That's life and full marks to the winner and the first three. I would love to have seen them on good to soft ground. They're key factors. Sometimes they work in your favour, sometimes they don't.'

Teddy Grimthorpe, racing manager to owner Khalid Abdullah, said there were no regrets over keeping Enable in training this year and spoke warmly about her remarkable contribution to the sport.

'Enable has given us so much, not only to Juddmonte and Prince Khalid but to the whole sport. She's been such an important part of our lives and we have no complaints nor excuses,' said Grimthorpe.

'It's us who try to push her to do things. She's happy and retained her enthusiasm. She loves racing, her routine, her life and Frankie too, just as he loves her. They have a wonderful relationship.

'The expectations surrounding her have been pretty enormous but she's been such a joy. For her to win a third King George this year was exceptional. She's got a truly extraordinary CV.'

6160a **QATAR PRIX DE L'ARC DE TRIOMPHE (GROUP 1) (3YO+) (GRANDE COURSE) (NO GELDINGS) (TURF)** **1m 4f**

3:05 3-Y-O+ **£1,452,711** (£581,186; £290,593; £145,169; £72,711)

			RPR
1		**Sottsass (FR)**^{22} 5381 4-9-5 0 .... Cristian Demuro 4 (J-C Rouget, France) *trckd ldrs: rdn 2f out: drvn over 1f out: led 1f out: kpt on wl fnl f: drvn out* **73/10**	123
2	*nk*	**In Swoop (IRE)**^{21} 5421 3-8-13 0 .... Ronan Thomas 1 (F-H Graffard, France) *midfield on inner: rdn and stdy hdwy fr over 2f out: drvn and styd on fnl f: nrst fin* **10/1**	122+
3	*1 3/4*	**Persian King (IRE)**^{28} 5153 4-9-5 .... Pierre-Charles Boudot 7 (A Fabre, France) *led: rdn ins fnl 2f: drvn over 1f out: hdd 1f out: kpt on* **63/10**^{3}	119
4	*hd*	**Gold Trip (FR)**^{21} 5421 3-8-13 0 .... Stephane Pasquier 9 (F Chappet, France) *hld up towards rr of midfield: stdy hdwy into midfield 3f out: rdn and effrt 2f out: hung rt ins fnl 2f: ev ch 1 1/2f out: no ex fnl 100yds* **33/1**	119+
5	*2*	**Raabihah (USA)**^{21} 5422 3-8-9 0 .... Maxime Guyon 2 (J-C Rouget, France) *hld up towards rr of midfield: rdn 2f out: swtchd towards outside 1 1/2f out: styd on fnl f* **13/1**	112+
6	*2*	**Enable**^{29} 5103 6-9-2 0 .... Frankie Dettori 5 (John Gosden) *in tch in midfield: trckd ldrs over 2f out: rdn ins fnl 2f: short of room and lost pl 1 1/2f out: kpt on same pce: no ex fnl 100yds* **9/10**^{1}	110
7	*1/2*	**Stradivarius (IRE)**^{21} 5423 6-9-5 0 .... Olivier Peslier 14 (John Gosden) *midfield on outside: tk clsr order 3f out: rdn 2f out: short of room and lost pl 1 1/2f out: no ex fnl f* **54/10**^{2}	112
8	*2 1/2*	**Deirdre (JPN)**^{66} 3828 6-9-2 0 .... Jamie Spencer 12 (Mitsuru Hashida, Japan) *s.s: in rr: rdn and kpt on fr 2f out: no further imp fnl f* **79/1**	105
9	*nse*	**Way To Paris**^{21} 5423 7-9-5 0 .... Ioritz Mendizabal 6 (Andrea Marcialis, France) *hld up towards rr of midfield: rdn and no imp fr 2f out* **46/1**	108
10	*3/4*	**Royal Julius (IRE)**^{14} 5696 7-9-5 0 .... Shane Foley 8 (J Reynier, France) *hld up towards rr: rdn and no imp fr over 2f out* **103/1**	107
11	*20*	**Chachnak (FR)**^{28} 5154 3-8-13 0 .... Tony Piccone 13 (F Vermeulen, France) *chsd ldr: rdn over 2f out: hmpd and squeezed out 1 1/2f out: sn btn: eased fnl f* **81/1**	75

2m 39.3s (8.90) **Going Correction** +0.975s/f (Soft)
WFA 3 from 4yo+ 6lb **11** Ran SP% **118.7**
Speed ratings: **109,108,107,107,106 104,104,102,102,102 88**
PARI-MUTUEL (all including 1 euro stake): WIN 8.30; PLACE 2.50, 3.10, 3.00; DF 19.30.
Owner White Birch Farm **Bred** Ecurie Des Monceaux **Trained** Pau, France

Eight days later Enable's glittering career – which included two Arcs, an Oaks, an Irish Oaks, three King Georges, a Breeders' Cup Turf, a Coral-Eclipse and two Yorkshire Oaks – was brought to an end.

Her trainer said: 'Enable has retired happy and sound after an extraordinary career. We here at Clarehaven Stables have been very fortunate to be with her for the past five years and to appreciate her strong character and athletic prowess.'

Teddy Grimthorpe added: 'She has brought so much joy to everyone who has been involved with her. Her elegance and forceful personality have been nurtured by John and his team at Clarehaven, especially by Imran [Shahwani] who has looked after her with such calm and devotion.

'Her CV withstands the closest of inspections, very few can match what she has given to racing.'

It was also revealed that Enable would join the Juddmonte broodmare band to be covered by Kingman, who has made a rapid ascent in the stallion standings since his own retirement, in 2021.

Enable's racing career was entwined with that of Dettori, and her greatest ally and fan paid an emotional tribute to the mare.

'It's been an amazing journey,' he said. 'The Arc this year unfortunately didn't work out. It was the worst performance of her career so I'm not surprised at the decision. She owes nobody anything, she's been an absolutely super mare.

'I did have a cry last night when I was told but more of joy than sadness because of all the great memories she gave me.'

Enable gave a generation of racing fans memories to last a lifetime. So, for that, we thank you and salute you.

ENABLE: AN APPRECIATION

by Peter Thomas

There's a concept in racing – let's call it 'the tyranny of the unbeaten horse' – that has a lot to answer for. In short, it dictates that an exciting youngster, having racked up the requisite (usually quite small) number of winning appearances, becomes less of a racehorse and more of a precious commodity to be shielded from undue risk and spared, if at all possible, the ignominy of defeat.

Perhaps it's because she's a mare, perhaps because she was (quite remarkably, with hindsight) beaten on her second start, but Enable was never wrapped in cotton wool. With one of the game's most enduringly sporting men as her owner and one of its most prescient trainers at the helm of her career, she was afforded the opportunity to establish beyond doubt the breadth and depth of her talent.

We discovered early on in her racing life that brilliance on the gallops and raw speed were not among her attributes – with Frankie Dettori bypassing her in favour of her more showy stablemate Shutter Speed for that Newbury loss in April 2017 – but the Italian soon realised where Enable's talents lay and he was on board at Chester when she began a staggering unbeaten sequence of 12 races that included ten Group 1 wins.

With experience under her belt, she proved herself to be not short of tactical speed – capable of dropping back in trip for an Eclipse when the occasion demanded and getting the job done with a minimum of fuss in 2019 – but it was in the thick of the middle-distance programme that she shone the brightest, and in that realm she accepted every challenge to her crown.

This wasn't an iron horse with impenetrable armour; minor injuries kept her off the track for two long and frustrating spells, after the first of which, in 2018, she was asked to dip into Group 3 company to reacquaint herself with the heat of competition. Even that day, however, she had to fend off the challenge of Crystal Ocean to keep her seam of achievement intact, and when restored to the top level she carried on as though nothing had happened.

Perhaps it was her psychological toughness, more so than any physical superiority, that set her apart from the herd. She had been a strapping, mature filly in her early days, but as that advantage diminished she was forced to dig deeper into the well of her mental constitution.

Where once she had stood apart quite simply as an athlete, her grinding victory over Crystal Ocean in the 2019 King George confirmed what she had already suggested: that when the going got tough and the tough got going, she had the wherewithal to put the tough firmly in their place.

She represented, quite simply, the essence of true grit in an arena that exerts demands barely comprehensible to those of us who don't spend our working lives among horses.

There was the occasional truly easy run, like that wholly deserved lap of honour at York in August 2019 – the one that tested Dettori's tear ducts far more than it tested Enable's resolve – but mostly Enable was asked serious questions wherever she was sent.

The laudable ambition of her connections ensured that hiding places were in short supply, no matter how expansive the world of international racing these days. Thus, she was asked to perform in the mud in Chantilly and on the unfamiliar terrain of Churchill Downs in Kentucky, she always gave of her best, and her best was normally sufficient.

Sadly, although not shamefully, the two days when she might have made her indelible mark in the history books were the two days when most went against her. In 2019, under an ambitious ride in a mud-spattered Arc, she was overhauled by a very good horse in Waldgeist; in 2020, having returned to the fray with a sole motive, she eventually found herself in conflict with the rain gods once again.

Defeat in the 2020 Eclipse had been of no great concern for a six-year-old with just one ambition; odds-on victory in the King George simply confirmed what we already knew and her cakewalk in the September Stakes was no more than a racecourse gallop to ensure her readiness for the first Sunday in October.

When constant rain ruled out her biggest rival Love, and feed irregularities removed the remainder of Aidan O'Brien's challenge for the Arc, it seemed as though fortune was finally beginning to favour the brave, but the rain refused to relent and by race time, the terrain was beyond what the French might call 'tres souple' and bordering on what we know as 'bottomless' – in short, no good for Enable, and in conjunction with a dawdling pace and a roughhouse of a contest, the end of her bid for history.

But what of it? Her sequence could have been protected; she could have been that mollycoddled mare with the flawless record; but that would have deprived us of so many magic moments.

If defeat was the price we had to pay for learning what a marvel had walked among us for four remarkable seasons, then so be it. Sixth place in her fourth Arc diminished not one iota the years of glory that went before.

Dettori said we'd have to go back to Brigadier Gerard to see her like, which was high praise indeed. He also said Enable had taken him to places his emotions had never been before, and that's surely the highest praise there is.

CAREER RECORD

ENABLE (GB)

12 February 2014 bay mare
Nathaniel (Ire) – Concentric (GB) (Sadler's Wells) (USA)
TRAINER: John Gosden
OWNER: Khalid Abdullah
BREEDER: Juddmonte Fams Ltd

Race record **1**/3111111/111/1112-21**1**6

LIFETIME RECORD

	RUNS	WINS	2NDS	3RDS	WINNINGS	EARNINGS	OR	BEST TS	BEST RPR
Flat	16	12	2	1	£9,564,984	£10,649,955	125	117	129
All-weather	3	3	0	0	£74,366	£74,366	125	102	126
Rules races	19	15	2	1	£9,639,350	£10,724,320	–	–	–

DATE	RACE CONDITIONS	WGT	RACE OUTCOME	JOCKEY	OR	TS	RPR
4 Oct 20	Lon 1m4fHy G1 1453K	9-2	6/11 (6¼L Sottsass 9-5) 9-10f	L Dettori	–	56	110
5 Sep 20	Kem 1m4fSt/Slw C1G3 32K	9-9	1/6 (7l Kirstenbosch 9-2) 1-14f	L Dettori	128	102	121
25 Jul 20	Asc 1m4f GF C1G1 227K	9-4	1/3 (5½L Sovereign 9-7) 4-9f	L Dettori	128	102	124
5 Jul 20	Sand 1m2f GF C1G1 142K	9-0	2/7 (2¼L Ghaiyyath 9-3) evnsf	L Dettori	128	106	121
6 Oct 19	Lon 1m4fVSft G1 2574k	9-2	2/12 (1¾l Waldgeist 9-5) 1-2f	L Dettori	–	115	123
22 Aug 19	Yor 1m4fGd C1G1 241k	9-7	1/4 (2¾l Magical 9-7) 1-4f	L Dettori	126	89	128
27 Jul 19	Asc 1m4fGS C1G1 709k	9-4	1/11 (nk Crystal Ocean 9-7) 8-15f	L Dettori	125	115	127
6 Jul 19	San 1m2fGF C1G1 425k	9-4	1/8 (¾l Magical 9-4) 4-6f L	L Dettori	125	105	124
3 Nov 18	Chu 1m4fGd G1 1630k	8-11	1/13 (¾l Magical 8-7) 8-13f	L Dettori	–	–	124
7 Oct 18	Lon 1m4fGd G1 2528k	9-2	1/19 (snk Sea Of Class 8-9) evnsf	L Dettori	–	114	122
8 Sep 18	Kem 1m4fSt/Sl C1G3 40k	9-2	1/4 (3½l Crystal Ocean 9-10) 8-15f	L Dettori	128	88	126
1 Oct 17	Cha 1m4fSft G1 2442k	8-9	1/18 (2½l Cloth Of Stars 9-5) 10-11f	L Dettori	–	116	129
24 Aug 17	Yor 1m4fGS C1G1 198k	8-12	1/6 (5l Coronet 8-12) 1-4f	L Dettori	126	102	124
29 Jul 17	Asc 1m4fGS C1G1 652k	8-7	1/10 (4½l Ulysses 9-7) 5-4f	L Dettori	122	117	128
15 Jul 17	Cur 1m4fGF 3yG1 198k	9-0	1/10 (5½l Rain Goddess 9-0) 2-5f	L Dettori	120	51	121
2 Jun 17	Eps 1m4fGd C13yG1 284k	9-0	1/9 (5l Rhododendron 9-0) 6-1	L Dettori	107	115	123
10 May 17	Chs 1m3½fGd C13yL 34k	9-0	1/7 (1¾l Alluringly 9-0) 2-1	L Dettori	102	82	111
21 Apr 17	Nby 1m2fGF C33y 10k	9-1	3/6 (2¾l Shutter Speed 9-1) 5-1	W Buick	84	79	103
28 Nov 16	Ncs 1mSt C52yMd 3k	9-0	1/9 (3¾l Gallifrey 9-0) 7-2	R Havlin	–	74	83

Following page: Enable is led into the parade ring before the King George